THE VISION PRINCIPLE

Discover Your Life Vision

Living a Life of Purpose, Passion, and Power
Finding Your Place in the Kingdom of God

Pastor Jack Irvin Sr.

www.thevisionprinciple.com

All scripture quotations are from the Authorized King James Version Special thanks to my wife Patty, for all her encouragement and my four children Marie, Jack Jr, Jenda, and Cassandra who have lived life with me for all these years. Thanks for all you have helped me along the way in writing and editing this book. You help has been invaluable.

The Vision Principle

ISBN 9781795833523

Genesis Companies LLC
158 Marvin Ave
Akron, Ohio 44302
2019

www.thevisionprinciple.com
email:pastorjack@thevisionprinciple.com

Genesis Companies LLC
158 Marvin Ave
Akron, Ohio 44302

Cover Design by Jenda Wight

Table of Contents

Introduction

Key Scripture: " *Where there is no vision the people perish.* " *(*Proverbs 29:18a*)*

Let me ask you a few questions? Are you yearning for a more fulfilled life? Do you feel you are living the life that God purposed for you to live? What passion burns in your soul that keeps you awake at night? Do you lack the power to accomplish what only you can do with the help of our Heavenly Father? In this book we will discuss these questions in great detail. This book is not intended for those who are not visionaries or lack the motivation to do great thing in their life. If you are the faint of heart and are happy with a mundane life, then this book is not for you. The book of Daniel describes "those who do great exploits for their God". Is it time for you to make a difference in other people's lives? Decide now to invest some time and energy in finding your God given life vision and being relentless in your pursuit of the plan God has for your life.

Years ago I was on a pastoral visitation and went to the house to see a couple who had been occasionally attending my church in Arizona. As I was invited into the home by the sister who answered the door, I noticed after a few minutes, her husband was not coming to the living room to greet me and the wife seemed a bit distracted. As I later found out, her husband was reluctant to come and meet me as he was not particularly interested in spiritual things. As the sister disappeared into another room for a short period of time, she came back in the living room and said, Pastor I need your help. My husband was afraid to come talk to you, so he tried to climb out the window in the bathroom and he got stuck. She asked me if I could help her get him unstuck. So I proceeded to the bathroom and sure enough he was stuck in a small window which he had tried to crawl out to avoid having to see me. I tried to not laugh and I assisted in helping him get unstuck, much to his chagrin. The good news is he later gave his heart to the Lord and became a devoted follower of Jesus.

Are you feeling stuck in life? Are you dissatisfied with status quo? Are you ready to live a life of vision, passion, purpose and power? Imagine waking up each day with excitement and vigor to pursue what the Lord has ordained for you each day.

Jesus said, *"I have come that you might have life, and life more abundantly." (**John 10:10**)*

Are you ready to let God fill you with His plan and purpose for your life? Is it time to reject a mediocre life and begin to dream the impossible, living your life in total obedience to His heavenly calling and vision?

In my travels around the country having shared with individuals, churches of all denominations, bible colleges and ministries, one consistent theme has emerged. There seems to be an epidemic among the Body of Christ, I would call this epidemic, hopelessness. Famous political, social, and religious institutions and familiar foundations that we have so often relied upon, have rapidly deteriorated. People seem to be motivated by fear and despair. Abuse of prescription drug use has skyrocketed. People are very dissatisfied with status quo and are looking for a more significant life. Shallow Christianity, a mile wide and an inch deep, although very popular, has left many believers unsatisfied and on a search for real meaning and significance to their lives. The American dream of owning a house and raising a family and keeping up with the Jones's has brought great frustration to many people. This great dream for many has turned into a nightmare with broken lives, large divorce rates, massive foreclosures and bankruptcies at an all time high. God has been doing us a great favor with all the upheaval around us in great institutions and religious foundations.

*" And this word, Yet once more, signifieth the removing of those things that are shaken , as of things that are made, that those things which cannot be shaken may remain ." (**Hebrews 12:27**)*

We have a Kingdom that can not be shaken. The institutions and systems that we have come to rely on in previous generations have been corroding and crumbling. Business failures, church scandals, government corruption and endless breakdowns in the things we have come to trust, have shaken the basic foundations of our society. What do we do to stem the tide of hopelessness in America and reverse despair in so many American lives? I believe the answer lies in Holy Scripture.

Do we understand the source of hope? Do we know the one who holds our future? Can we get back to what is really important and bring a real sense of passion, purpose and power back into our lives? The answer I believe is yes.

A few years ago, I started my 6th decade in this life and have come to the realization thru many failures, frustrations and attempts at making sense of life, that I want to help as many people as possible get off the great American nightmare and get on the train bound with Hope and Glory led by our conductor, King of Kings and Lord of Lords, Jesus Christ our Redeemer. As Christians we understand how to get to Heaven, but we possess very little understanding of how we are ambassadors for another Kingdom which is not of this earth. We are representatives of our King from heaven, to demonstrate to this world the manifold wisdom of God. Godly wisdom is simply having special insight into the things of God from His perspective, seeing thru the eyes of eternity. God has an awesome heavenly plan for our lives.

As Paul's prayed in **Ephesians 1:16-23** he clearly demonstrates the importance of wisdom. *"That he might give us the spirit of wisdom,"* (special insight from God's point of view).

How would you like to live a life of passion and purpose, trusting in the power of God to accomplish great things for His Kingdom. I want to help get you out of the doldrums and help put you on a path of excitement with new energy to be all your heavenly Father has created you for. No this is not another self help, get rich quick, new age attempt to get you side tracked. This is an attempt to put your life back on track to the heartbeat of God. Yes, He holds your future, you are in the palm of His hand. He is your creator and He wants you to use the creativity that He has given you to live life to its fullest. I call this the Vision Principle. Let me attempt to explain what I mean by this principle.

The word for vision in Hebrew is *Chazown* which simply means dream /perception/ revelation.

Delight thyself also in the Lord; and he shall give thee the desires of thine heart. **(Psalm 37:4)**

If we delight in him, he will give us the desires of our heart. The root word for desire comes from two different words, *de and sire.* Simply stated this means **Of the Father.** In order to understand the Vision Principle, we must understand the source of our creativity, and our God given dream/ vision, so we can live our lives out of passion, purpose and power. Everything starts with God. In the beginning was God. Genesis 1:1 All three areas of passion, purpose and power are vital to understand in helping you pursue the one who freely gives us all things for us to enjoy.We must get off the bandwagon of selfishness and self centeredness, attempting to find fulfillment in selfish ambition and things which were not designed to give us real deep satisfaction.We need God's wisdom from an eternal perspective, realizing that God's wants us to get to our final destination of Heaven but also that we represent in this life to a lost and dying world that our Father who is in Heaven has a better plan than we do.

Wherefore holy brethren, partakers of the heavenly calling, consider the Apostle and High Priest of our profession, Christ Jesus. *(Hebrews 3:1)*

Saints we have a heavenly calling just like Jesus and Paul. Paul as he was brought before Agrippa, stated in Acts, *I was not disobedient to the heavenly vision.* The desires I am talking about are God's desires (of the Father) which he has placed in our redeemed hearts, for us to function according to His plan and pattern. God has given us a vision / dream that he has placed in our hearts, that He alone has planned for us to walk in all our days. Are you searching for that dream? Can you stop and invest some time in making sense of your life? What is your passion? What is the real purpose of your life here on earth? Are you operating with the real power that God supplies when we are in a real relationship with Him? Come with me on this journey. Take some time to investigate the dream that God has given you and you alone. Let me help you sort out God's design for your life, knowing our time is short. Come discover how the Vision Principle can help transform your life. Vision is a function of the new heart we receive when we are born again in Christ. **The Vision Principle is simply living life from our God given vision which our creator has designed for us, walking in His power and purpose living from a passionate heart redeemed by Jesus**. He has placed His vision in our redeemed hearts to motivate us to do His will.

Without vision people perish. (Proverbs 29:18)

Let me ask you a question. Do you know where to start? This book will help you in pursuit of your heavenly vision, one of God's creation. In this book, we will attempt to show the power and effect a clear concise vision can have on our daily lives. The eagle as it soars above the earth normally all alone, has a tremendous ability to see afar when needed. We also need to soar to the heavens to clearly see what God has ordained for our lives. As we look to Jesus, *the author and the finisher of our faith*, we will begin to understand our destiny and purpose. Eagles have incredible vision and as stated in **Job 39:29** , *can see afar off.*

Let me remind you that there are two types of visions. One is from God, and one is from some other source other than God, such as selfish ambition, or deceit from the enemy. We can have a self centered false vision or a God given vision. God is the initiator and source of all vision. Jesus said that I only do what I see the father do.

Whereupon, O King Agrippa, I was not disobedient unto the heavenly vision . (Acts 26:19)

God is the author of our life vision. Any other source of vision is not complete or satisfying. Sometimes it takes an entire lifetime to find out this is true. Ezekiel chapters 12 and 13 clearly show the two types of vision, a true vision or a false vision. In chapter 12 God gives Ezekiel a true vision that will befall his people and He tells him that this will come to pass quickly. In Ezekiel 13, the Lord rebukes the false prophets who have spoken lies to the people of God,

Have ye not seen a vain vision, and have ye not spoken a lying vain divination, whereas ye say, The LORD saith it; albeit I have not spoken? **(Ezekiel 13:6)**

A false vision is self centered and a true vision will benefit others.

A false vision will not satisfy, a true vision will brings satisfaction.

A false vision will not come to pass, a true vision will be completed.

A false vision comes from us, a true vision comes from God.

Remember the seed of your true vision has been place inside you by God. Although your current vision might be in seed form, if you decide to invest in your relationship with God, you can certainly discover that seed growing into a forest with fresh life. It is your responsibility to discover and develop your vision. Purpose in your heart to devote your life to discovering, developing and experiencing your God given vision. Today is the day of salvation.

Each chapter has a key statement, key scripture, and key question. Also at the end of each chapter there will be application and action questions. There will also be at the end of each chapter, a general prophetic word from the Lord birthed in my prayer time for those who would read the book. We also have available a study guide which can be used in a small group setting or Bible study. There are links in various locations in the book to provide extra tools that will assist you in practical things you can do to discover, develop and experience your God given vision, so you can live by the Vision Principle.

Understanding The Kingdom of God

In order to understand and operate in the Vision Principle we must clearly understand how the Kingdom of God operates. Scripture give us some basic principles of how the Kingdom of God or the Kingdom of Heaven operates. In all the discussions and books written on the Kingdom of God, I am clearly not taking about us taking over the world and ushering in the reign of Christ. I am not talking about us chasing things of this world in order to be satisfied with what we possess. I am talking about us being in submission to the King in His rule and character, seeking first the Kingdom of God and His righteousness.

But seek ye first the kingdom of God, and his righteousness; and all these things shall be added unto you. **(Matthew 6: 33)**

We are to submit to His Lordship and let Him live thru us, so we reflect His nature. All we will ever accomplish and all we will ever be, must be a reflection of the King and His rule in our hearts. We must understand the Kingdom of God is all about the heart. Not trying to bring people in subjection to us, but to display a Christ like life for all to see the nature of our King, the Lord Jesus and His wonderful love for us. God's Kingdom is within us. We are to influence this world, not control it.

Neither shall they say, lo here! or lo there for, behold the kingdom of God is within you. **(Luke 17:21)**

God's Kingdom always starts from the inside out. Religion emphasizes the external, God's Kingdom emphasizes the internal in our hearts first, then His Kingdom is displayed to express the love of the Father to those whom He wants to redeem from the snares of the enemy. Vision is a function of the heart not of our natural sight. We can see with our eyes in the natural but not really understand what we are seeing. This is not vision. The Kingdom of God starts with our relationship to God when we are born again. We must understand that we display the Kingdom of God everywhere we go. The Kingdom is much bigger than Church. When we walk in the Kingdom, we should have an everywhere focus. We are His ambassadors reflecting what our King is like. Your vision from God will have a Kingdom focus which always initiates with seeking first the King and His righteousness (Matthew 6:33) This helps us stay on task and not get distracted with other things that are not very important.

One of the most important keys in the Kingdom is the key of revelation from the heart of God to our hearts. In the parable of the sower found in Matthew Chapter 13, Jesus tells His disciples the story of the sower, sowing seed in four types of ground. The ground is a picture of the heart and the seed a picture of the word of God. The condition of the heart is the key to bringing forth fruit, some hundredfold, sixtyfold, some thirtyfold. God's revelation is given to us in our redeemed hearts so we can understand His plan and purpose.

For this people's heart is waxed gross, and theirs ears are dull of hearing, and their eyes they have closed; lest at anytime they should see with their eyes and hear with their ears, and should understand with their heart, and should be converted, and I should heal them. **(Matthew 13:15)**

Let me remind you that God has given us a new heart when we are born again. This is part of the New Covenant of grace we receive as His children in the Kingdom of God. The New Covenant gives us an inheritance that is eternal.

And for this cause he is the mediator of the new testament, that by means of death, for the redemption of the trangressions that were under the first testament, they which are called might receive the promise of eternal inheritance. **(Hebrews 9:15)**

Our ultimate vision from God must have a Kingdom focus in order to be properly aligned with His purposes. We seek first His Kingdom and all the other things in life will be added as needed. God reveals His plans to us in our hearts that are in tune with Him and sensitive to the leading of His Holy Spirit. In the Kingdom, being in right relationship with the King is the first step in finding and fulfilling your vision. If we have a great ministry but we are not like Jesus, we are poor ambassadors for our King. Being is more important than doing, when we are walking out our vision. We can accomplish many great things in this life, but if we are not like Jesus, it is all in vain. Another scripture in the Gospel of Matthew shows us the importance of having a heart that understands.

He answered and said unto them, Because it is given unto you to know the mysteries of the kingdom of Heaven, but to them it is not given. (Matthew 13:11)

The word mysteries in greek is the word *mysterion* and it simply means hidden or secret thing.

God wants us to know the secret things and plans that He has for us in His heart. The key to knowing secret things of importance, is our relationship with the King in a personal relationship that is submitted to His rule. Many motivational speakers, who I am sure have good intentions for the most part, many times call this energy or karma. This is a self-help and self-centered approach to life. Do not be conformed to the things in this world with a man centered approach. This will be a disaster for your life. Yes there is power within us, but when we are born again from above, this power is clearly from our creator and heavenly father and His name is Jesus, King of Kings and Lord of all. Our Father knows what is best for us and He wants to reveal His awesome plan for our lives, as we seek Him first as King. He has given us His righteousness as a precious gift when we enter His Kingdom.

But as it is written, Eye hath not seen, nor ear heard, neither have entered into the heart of man, the things which God hath prepared for them that love him. But God hath revealed them unto us by his Spirit: for the Spirit searcheth all things, yea the deep things of God. (1 Corinthians 2:9-10)

God is shifting things in the earth from the Body of Christ being church centered to Kingdom centered. The church should not just be a building, but a training ground to equip the saints to operate in the Kingdom. Jesus told us the Kingdom of God is within you. A

Kingdom minded church or believer has an everywhere focus. The Vision Principle is written to help you operate in the Kingdom, not just church. Let me share just a few more principles on the Kingdom of God. There are so many principles that it would take another entire book to cover these. A simple definition of the Kingdom of God is: *the rule and reign of King Jesus over His citizens who bring the culture of His character and rule and carry out His will and purpose over their sphere of influence or field.* Below are just a few principles we need to understand about the Kingdom;

- The Kingdom of God is all about the King. (Matthew 6:33)

- The Kingdom of God must be demonstrated. (1 Corinthians 4:20)

- The Kingdom of God is focused on bringing heaven to earth. (Matthew 6:10)

- The Kingdom of God is within you. (Luke 17:21)

- The Kingdom of God operates properly in your God called field. (Matthew 13:24)

- The Kingdom of God is entered through much tribulation. (Romans 14:22)

- The Kingdom of God has influence and growth, not control. (Matthew13:31-33)

- The Kingdom of God language is love. (1 Corinthians 13)

- The Kingdom of God has a door which is humility. (Matthew 23:11-13)

- The Kingdom of God has a territory, subjects, laws, and a ruler. (Matthew 6:33)

HELPFUL RESOURCES

Kingdom Shift by Sunday Adelaja
Ekklesia by Ed Silvoso

....

Chapter 1
Personal Relationship Brings Purpose

Key Scripture : **Nehemiah 1:1** *The words of Nehemiah the son of Hachaliah*

Relationship with God our creator is the starting point for vision. Everything starts with God. *In the beginning was God.* **(Genesis 1:1)**

As we develop our relationship with our creator, we begin to discover who He is and ultimately find who we are. In our journey through life, we find our particular vision when we have a vision of what God is really like. We must know what He is like so we can know what we are to be like. Understanding God's ultimate purpose for our lives is paramount to understanding what our life vision should be. God's ultimate primary purpose for our lives is found in a famous portion of scripture in **Romans 8:28-29** . In this portion of Scripture we find God's general purpose for all our lives in a verse we often quote but sometimes do not understand. We all have heard the verse God works all things out for our good for those who love him and are called according to his purpose. The next verse clearly describes what God's purpose is for all of us in general sense.

For whom he did foreknow, he also did predestinate to be conformed to the image of his Son, that he might be the firstborn among many brethren. ***(Romans 8:29)***

God's general purpose for all believers is that we would be like Jesus (conformed to His image.)

When the Lord made man he said,"*Let us make man in our image and likeness.*" ***(Genesis 1:26)***

Obviously after the fall of man, sin distorted our image and we began to experience life without a right relationship with God. Jesus came to restore us back to His life and image. *2 Corinthians 3:18* Paul describes us being transformed into the image as we are beholding of the Glory of God as in a mirror. We look in the mirror to see who God is and we begin to see who He has made us to be in Christ. We are learning to be like the new creation He has made us to be.

Our image of who God is will determine who we think we are. If our view of the image of God is distorted, then our view of who we will become, will be distorted. Your heavenly Father is the kindest, most awesome person to ever be. He is not like anyone we have ever known. But this view of the image of God only comes through divine revelation brought by Jesus as we walk in relationship to him. God has an image of you, can you see it.? He sees you whole and walking in His fullness and in His completeness. This is the essence of our vision God has for our lives. If our image of God is not accurate, then the image of ourselves will not be accurate.

In the book of Nehemiah we see some great principles for finding, developing and living in your vision. Nehemiah (means Jehovah comforts). He was in a relationship with God who gave him comfort upon hearing terrible news about his people who were living in Jerusalem without any walls of protection. Nehemiah was in a place in his life where he wanted to go back home to help his people. He lived in captivity in the palace at Shushan as he was the cupbearer of King Artaxerxes, a Persian King whose kingdom had taken over from the Babylonians. After hearing the bad news about his brothers, even at the risk of his own life, he had a burden from the Lord to help his fellow Jews. Many times our specific purpose will begin to surface when we are at a place in our lives where we would rather not be. God has a way of making us uncomfortable so we will begin to pursue Him. He created us with the purpose of us being conformed to His image and has placed in us a specific assignment only we can carry out. As we develop our relationship with God, we begin to discover our specific purpose or vision for our lives. Purpose is another word to describe God's will for our lives. The number one question that I have been asked as a Pastor is, "what is God's will for my life."Another definition for purpose would be God's original intent. God knew your purpose before he every created you. Only God knows your purpose for your life. He wants you to not only know His will, but to also walk in His will.

Before I formed thee in the belly I knew thee; and before thou camest forth out of the womb I sanctified thee and ordained thee a prophet to the nations. (Jeremiah 1:5)

We will find purpose as we develop intimacy with our heavenly Father. Intimacy with God leads us to discover our identity in God. We must first have a vision of who God is before we begin to understand who we are in God. In modern times people describe God in many ways, but in reality they many times are their own God. God has given us a clear picture of who He is in the person of Jesus Christ. Jesus left the glories of heaven and came to earth, humbled himself and became one of us to show us what God is like. He clearly said, *if you have seen me, you have seen the father.*

Jesus saith unto him, I am the way, the truth, and the life: no man cometh unto the Father but by me.(John 14:6)

Therefore *if any man be in Christ, he is a new creature:old things are passed away; behold,all things are become new. (2 Cor 5:17)*

Surprise

When we receive Christ, we receive a new identity and a new relationship with God. Jesus is the only way for us to come to the Father. Have you committed your life to Jesus? He is patiently waiting. Surrender today to His control. Your relationship with Him will be the key to discovering your life vision. All your problems will not fade away instantly, but the good news is you will have the one who can help you through your problems with His peace and power. I got a great surprise right after my conversion that was quite unexpected. I gave my heart to the Lord at the age of 9. Little did I know that a few days after my salvation, I would experience an unusual event. I got kidnapped and was held for several hours before being rescued. It had been a usual day where four kids, my brother and two of my best friends, were simply out on a bike ride. We had jumped up on the freeway that was still under construction near our houses to ride our bikes. We only had two bikes so we were share riding with two on each bike. We somehow got separated and my friend Terry and I ended up walking home while my brother and one of my friends kept riding the bikes. We started to head back to our houses, so we got off the newly constructed freeway and begin to walk underneath the freeway bridge. We immediately came to one of Houston's famous bayous and we could not cross because of the height of the water, as neither one of us could swim. We turned around and immediately a man grab us and tied us up under the bridge. He had a big German Shephard dog, that he used to paralyze us with fear to keep us from running off. He took all our paper route money and kept us for several hours, beating us and trying to molest us. After a few hours my brother and mother found us and we were delivered. They never did find the man. That was a dark and dreary day in Texas, but Jesus was with me and gave me supernatural peace even as a young child. We will not be exempt from challenging issues, but Jesus will be our anchors in the midst of the storms in this life.

As we spend time in intimacy with Jesus, we begin to find out who He really is. We then in turn find out who we are in Christ. A life without a relationship with God is a life that has very little meaning. We need to be in tune with the one who created us with a plan and purpose. Purpose is the answer to the why of your life. Why are you here? When Jesus was physically on earth he understood His purpose.

For this purpose was the Son of God manifested, that he might destroy the works of the devil. (1 John 3:8)

In the same chapter of 1 John in verse 5 we also see specifically why Jesus was manifested, *(to take away our sins; and in him is no sin.)* He completed His assignment and took away our sin, destroying the control of the devil and releasing us from the condemnation and accusation he brings. We have a new identity now in Christ, we are saints, separated unto God for His purpose. Jesus knew He was born to go to the cross to destroy the works of the devil. We too, need to know why we are here on earth. God has place inside of us His seed, the incorruptible word of God with His purpose and plan for our lives. We must nurture and cultivate that seed in order for it to grow into what God has planned. Remember every forest starts with a small seed and develops into an awesome forest. Scripture declares what the Kingdom of Heaven is like. In Matthew 13, the smallest seed, a mustard seed grows into the greatest among herbs, so that the birds of the air come and lodged in the branches there-of. God wants you to grow into the full stature of Christ unto a mature man. Take some time to make some declarations of who you believe God wants you to be. Both Jesus and Paul were clear on the work they were called to do. We likewise should have clarity as to what God has called us to do.

I have glorified thee on the earth: I have finished the work which thou gavest me to do. **(John 17:4)**

As they ministered to the Lord, and fasted, the Holy Ghost said, Separate me Barnabas and Saul for the work whereunto I have called them. **(Acts 13:2)**

Years ago, there was a very wealthy man, who with his devoted son, loved to collect priceless art. They would travel around together and purchase only the finest treasures they could find for their collection.The works would include works by Van Gogh, Picasso, Monet and many other famous artist. The widowed older man, developed a great love for his son and his ability to find great works of art. Over the years they drew extremely close together and the Father had great satisfaction as his son was a great art collector. As winter approached, war engulfed the nation, and the young man left to serve his country. After a short period of time, the father received a telegram that his son was missing in action. The father anxiously awaited more news, fearing he would never see his son again. His fears were confirmed, as he received word his son had died rushing a wounded soldier to the medic. The father was brokenhearted and facing the upcoming time of Christmas with much anguish and sadness without the presence of his son. On Christmas morning a knock on the door awakened the man. As he walked to the door the masterpieces of all the art reminded him of his beloved son. As he opened the door, he was greeted by a soldier with a large package in his hand. He introduced himself to the father by saying, " I was a friend of your son." I was the one he was rescuing when he died. May I come in for a few moments? I have something to show you. As the two began to talk, the friend mentioned how the son had told everyone how much his father and him had loved fine art. I'm an artist the soldier said, and I want to give you this. As the old man unwrapped the package, the paper gave way to reveal a portrait of the son. The picture captured in great detail, the features of the son's face. Overcome with emotion, the father promised the soldier he would hang the portrait over the fireplace. After the soldier had left, the Father commenced to hang the portrait of his son over the fireplace pushing aside other masterpieces which seem insignificant compared to the portrait of his son. The man spent the rest of Christmas gazing at his son's painting. After days and weeks the father realized that he would not see his son again but he would live on as he gazed to the portrait. More and more stories surfaced of the young mans heroics, as he had rescued many soldiers before a bullet ended his caring heart. The painting of his son became his most prize possession of all the priceless art he possessed. He told his neighbors it was the greatest gift he had ever received.

The following spring the old man became ill and died. The art world was in anticipation. According to the will of the father, all those paintings would be sold at an auction on Christmas day. The day arrived and art lovers from around the world gathered to bid on some of the world's most spectacular paintings. The auction began with a painting that was not on the auctioneers list. It was a painting of the man's son. The auctioneer asked for an opening bid. The room was silent. Who will open the bidding with $100 ? Minutes passed and no one spoke. From the back of the room came, "Who cares about that painting." It is just a picture of his son. Let's forget about it and go on to the good stuff." Many other voices echoed in agreement. "No, we have to sell this one first replied the auctioneer. Now who will take the son?" Finally a friend of the old man spoke. "Will you take ten dollars for the painting?" That's all I have. I knew the boy, so I'd like to have it." "I have ten dollar, will anyone go higher? called the auctioneer." After more silence the auctioneer said, "going once, going twice, gone." The gavel fell, cheers filled the room and someone exclaimed, "now we can get on with it and we can bid on the treasures." The auctioneer looked at the audience and announced the auction was over. Stunned disbelief quieted the room. Someone spoke up, "What do you mean it is over? We didn't come here for a picture of some old guy's son. What about all these paintings? There are millions of dollars of art here. I demand an explanation." The auctioneer replied,"it is very simple, according to the will of the father, whoever takes the son, gets it all.

In this story is an important lesson for all of us. The Father loved his son and he gave him for all of us, so that we could enter into a loving relationship with him through Jesus Christ." *He that gets the son get it all."* When we enter God's kingdom we receive an inheritance that is priceless. God has come to live in us and give us all things we need to accomplish His will and purpose. In His kingdom we have an unlimited supply to all we will ever need.

The Lord of hosts hath sworn, saying, Surely as I have thought, so shall it come to pass; and as I have purposed, so shall it stand. **(Isaiah 14:24)**

The late Dr. Myles Munroe, in his book, *The Pursuit of Purpose*, make this statement,"*Purpose is the master motivation and mother of commitment. It is the source of enthusiasm and the womb of perseverance. Purpose gives birth to hope and instills the passion to act."* When we have enthusiasm for what we are doing in life, we have a vibrancy that is attractive to all around us.The root meaning of the word enthusiasm is to be *in God.* We as true believers, are in Christ and we should be the most enthusiastic people on the face of the earth. Understand today that God wants you to fulfill His purpose in the time you are on this earth. Start the journey and begin to pursue His purpose with all your heart.Talk to Him and listen with an open heart. He will guide you into all truth.

One helpful question to ask yourself is what are you called? What is your profession that you sense is your calling. If you had a title, what would you be called? Paul was a preacher, teacher and apostle in 2 Timothy 1:11. Paul also describes himself in Romans 1:1, Paul a servant of Jesus Christ, called to be an apostle. He knew his mission. If you could describe your self in the descriptions listed below, what title or profession would you give yourself in the future when you are fulfilling your God given assignment.

Circle at least one or possibly more:

Pastor	Teacher	Business Man
Apostle	Author Entrepreneur	Minister
Trainer	Church	Consultant Life
Coach	Prophet	Evangelist
Movie Maker	Corporate Trainer	Counselor
Engineer	Nurse Counselor	Seminar
Speaker	Discipler	Encourager
Writer	Father	Engineer
Nurse	Doctor	Mother

Other not listed: _____

This exercise will help you understand your purpose. Do not be afraid to ask someone else who knows you well and is spiritually mature to describe you in the future. Do not ask the dream killers. You know who those are.

Key Question
Have you answered the question, why am I here on earth?

_____

_____

_____

Action and Application.

Have you made a personal commitment to God by receiving Jesus Christ as His provision for both eternal and abundant life? If you have not done this, take some time right now to give your heart and life to Jesus. Find someone to share this with.

_____

_____

Write down several descriptions in one word, who you are becoming in Christ. We are complete in Him, growing up unto Him.

_____

_____

_____

Have you grown distant in your relationship with your Heavenly Father? It is time to draw near to Him again, and begin to discover the exciting plan He has for your life. Spend some time with Him alone and let Him clarify your vision. Write down what He says.

_____

_____

_____

Prophetic Word: *I have a purpose for you that was in my mind before I created you. Draw near to me and I will show you my perfect plan for your life. Let me be the source of your direction as I will lead you down the right path.*

HELPFUL RESOURCES

Pursuit of Purpose by Myles Munroe
On Purpose by Tamara Lowe

Chapter 2

Pain the Birthplace of our Assignment.

Key Scripture : Nehemiah 1:4 *And it came to pass, when I heard these words, that I sat down and **wept and mourned** certain days, and fasted, and prayed before the God of heaven.*

Nehemiah was in the palace of King Artaxerxes in Shushan, a place he did not want to be. Shushan was the winter palace for Artaxerxes King of Persia. The Medo-Persians had taken over from the Babylonians, who had taken the children of Israel captive to a foreign land. The Medo- Persians were now the rulers of a vast territory. Many times when we are in a place we would rather not be, it can cause us to cry out to God to make some changes. These changes can include our circumstances. Other times the changes will be internal. Changes can come inside of us in how we respond to the circumstances we find ourselves in.This is many times a good place to be.

Every vision will include an answer to a problem

Every problem and pain we experience in this life can sometime be quite challenging. This pain, although not to our liking, is the actual birthplace to our future assignment from God.

What is the greatest pain you are dealing with from your past? We must understand, we learn obedience through the things we suffer. Jesus went through the same things when He was on earth.

*Thou he were a Son, yet he learned obedience by the things which he suffered. **(Hebrews 5:8)***

Are you avoiding and hiding from this pain or confronting your pain with the healing, delivering power of God to make you whole? You see the pain we overcome, not avoid, can be the birthplace for our assignment. When Nehemiah heard the news of the devastation of Jerusalem and the state of his brothers he was overwhelmed with sadness. This was the starting point for his eventual assignment. But he did not remain in a state of sadness, but he began to let this pain be the springboard for his future ministry. In my own ministry and life, I have experienced many painful situations of all types, but one particular pain seems to jump out at this time in my life. This pain comes from the many years of ministry in corporate and private settings. Ministry in manufacturing plants, marketplaces, churches, schools, jails, and homes. The pain of seeing an empty look on the faces of people, both Christians and Non-Christians, who have no clue about their purpose or vision in this life. This look is sometimes overwhelming, as I see the emptiness deep down in their eyes which is a reflection of their souls being in deep despair. Ephesians Chapter 4 addresses this problem.

This I say therefore, and testify in the Lord, that ye henceforth walk not as other Gentiles walk in the vanity of their minds. *(Ephesians 4:17)*

If you study the word vanity, which is sometimes translated futility, you will come to understand the word has its root in a word that was used years ago, which is the word vagrancy. This is the official word used by governments to describe a transient or someone who is homeless. This word brings the idea of a person walking in a circle and never going in a direction that takes them someplace. I remember a specific day years ago, we were grocery shopping and as I went outside to sit down on a bench and let my family finish shopping, there was a man seated right outside the door and he looked homeless and quite unkept. I felt led to talk to him and I asked him, *how are you doing.*? He had that same empty look on his face that I have seen hundreds of time in churches and the marketplace, a look of despair. He answered me with these words, *not too good.* As I began to talk to him, he began to describe his life, which had been quite challenging, as his wife and kids had left him and he had not seen his family in years. During the conversation he told me how old he was and to my shock he was my exact age in his thirties. Life had taken it's toll on him and he looked at least 60 plus. I gave him a small amount of money and prayed for him as my family came out of the store. His painful past experiences had led to his current situation. We must understand that many of us have gone through similar devastating experiences but it did not destroy our lives. What is the difference? One is a victim and the other is a victor. Both have the same experience, but each reacts in a different way. Are you living your life as a victim or a victor? You need to make a choice. Do not be deceived into thinking you have had it a lot worse than everyone else. In most cases this is not true. Many that have the same tragic experience as the homeless man, have become overcomers with the help of Jesus. We can now use those experiences to ministry to people who are going through the same deep trials and tribulations. The Lord will use these experiences to mold us into His image. We as believers are not exempt from pain in this life. Although very difficult, these pains can be the birthplace of our vision.

Confirming the souls of the disciples, and exhorting them to continue in the faith, and that we must through much tribulation enter the kingdom of God (Acts 14:22)

Is your life like that man who was homeless ? Do you feel like your life is going in circles?

Stop and be honest with your self. Begin to look to your relationship with Jesus. He wants you to be an overcomer. We all will experience many trials and tribulations in this life, as that is how we enter the Kingdom of God. What pain have you experienced in your life that you have learned from, that you can use to help those in current problems? Nehemiah was distraught over the condition of his remnant brothers back in Jerusalem. After prayer and fasting he was willing to risk his life to bring help to those in a bad situation. If a cupbearer of the King showed sadness in the presence of the King, he could very easily be executed. Nehemiah was overwhelmed with a sense of vision even at the risk of his very life. Do you have a sense of purpose for your life that stays with you each and everyday, that keeps burning in your soul?

The Scream

None of us are exempt from pain in this life. I am sure you have had your part in painful experiences. I remember as a boy of 5 years old, a scream that is forever etched in my mind. It was a typical sunny day in the Houston area when suddenly things changed. The scream I had heard was from my mom. Unknown to me, were the events that were unfolding at our house as my Dad pulled into the driveway from a long day of work. My younger brother Randy as a two year old was excited to see my Dad and he took a broom and unlatched the two latches on the back screen door, so he could run out and see my Dad. In Texas the old screen doors were quite popular in the 50's. As he ran out with excitement to see his father, my Dad had no idea he was in the driveway. My Dad would pull his butane truck into the driveway, and then he would back up the last section and park on the side of the driveway. As he was backing up the truck, he ran over Randy and instantly killed him. My mom began to look for Randy and as she went outside I could hear the scream come from my mom that was quite startling. Thankfully I was not allowed to go outside and personally experience this tragedy that my mom and dad would live with the rest of their lives. Over the years, I got to watch two different responses from that tragic day in my mother and father. Later in life, having my own four children, I can not imagine the grief they had to live with each day of their lives. My mom dealt with this much better than my Dad. Understandably Dad was never quite the same from that day forward. He was filled with much frustration and anger that seem to express itself in how he treated others. He had a difficult time expressing his feelings and dealing with his immense pain. My mom used her strong faith to overcome this great pain. I watched her go through her own personal transformation overcoming an unbelievable difficult situation. But the story does not end here.

Almost 25 years later in Ohio, after I was married and had my own family, my son and I went to the bank to withdraw some money. We had a large Ford station wagon and on our way to the bank, my

2 year old Son crawled into the back seat and went to sleep. At that time there were no laws requiring safety seats. As I pulled up to the bank, I parked the car across the street and looked back at Jack Jr. who was sound asleep. I foolishly decided to not wake him up as the bank ATM machine was only about 15 feet away from my car. I took out the needed money and I turned around to go back to my car and the car was gone. I was immediately filled with terror. This terror was greater than anything, I had ever experienced. In my younger years I had been kidnapped, robbed twice, been in awful fights, but nothing compared to the fear I felt when I looked up and my car was gone with my 2 year old son inside. I crossed the street and literally grabbed two guys who were walking across the walkway and asked them quite forcefully, where is my son. They both immediately tried to calm me down and they said maybe your car rolled down the hill. I had parked the car on the side of the road, which had a steep hill with a 150 foot drop. I began to run down the hill for about a half a block with my heart racing and filled with unbelievable fear, wondering what happened to my son. As I got near to the bottom of the hill, I saw my car and there was no movement. The car had rolled down the steep hill, over an embankment and it was headed to the Grand River. A small tree next to a building near the river stopped the momentum of the car. As I approached the car, I saw no movement and I began to expect the worse. The station wagon had extensive damage. All of a sudden a woman appeared out from behind the building, carrying my son, who had a big smile on his face. Jack Jr. had no visible injuries at all. My panic and fear left and the overwhelming joy of seeing Jack Jr., almost caused me to pass out with relief. I grabbed Jack Jr. and held him tight, experiencing probably the greatest relief only a parent could feel, knowing your child was ok. I never did see the woman again to thank her, as I wonder if she was an angel sent from God to rescue Jack Jr.

After dealing with the police at the scene of the accident, I called home to tell my wife what had happened and I would need a ride home as the car was not driveable. The story does not end here, but takes a very unusual twist. After many years of not seeing my Dad, on this day he was visiting us from Texas. He was in the final stages of his life and he wanted to visit his boys in Ohio, as he was having serious heart problems. When I had called home, my wife put my Dad on the phone and I asked him to come get us. After all the legal issues were done with the police due to the accident, he picked us up and brought us back home. I had not seen my Dad in many years due to his abusive nature. I was developing my preaching skills at a local church and had been really pressing into God's perfect will for my life. I had developed a forgiving heart toward my Dad, and was glad to see him, not really knowing he was having severe heart trouble.When we arrived home, I could not see my Dad anywhere in the house, so I went outside and found him inside my detached garage. As I approached him, I could see he was crying. This was very unusual, as I had never seen my Dad cry before. Instantly I knew what was happening, he was having a flashback to 25 years before when he had accidentally ran over Randy at the age of two and killed him. Jack Jr. was two, Randy was two, was history repeating itself. Then something supernatural happened, that only God could orchestrate in this life. Imagine standing before the one who had abused your mother and you with an opportunity to represent the love of Jesus and the power of forgiveness. Would you be up for the challenge? I immediately put my arms around my Dad and told him, Dad you are forgiven, you could not have done anything different on the day Randy was killed. You are forgiven by God and I forgive you. God took an incredible painful experience from my Dad's life and even used a day in my life to bring healing to my Dad. He had lived with the awful pain and tragedy of losing a son 25 years before. Are you willing to let God use your pain, to help someone else overcome their pain? God heals us so we can bring healing to others. God redeems our mistakes, and bring His incredible mercy and forgiveness.

It is of the Lord's mercies that we are not consumed, because his compassions fail not. They are new every morning:great is thy faithfulness.(Lamentations 3:21-22)

The Smell

On a typical cool sunny day in the waterfront area of Houston, Texas, I was on my way home on the bus ride from junior high school as a thirteen year old teenager. Arriving home, as I walked into my house, I could smell a very strange odor that I had never smelled before. There was no one home, as my mom was at work and my older brother and sister were not home from school yet, or at least I thought. All at once a neighbor next door came running quite frantically, saying they took Donna to the hospital, she fell into the space heater. Needless to say, I was filled with great fear and uncertainty. Back in those days there were no cell phones, so I had no way to communicate with my brother or my mom. I ran next door to the tavern where my mom worked as she was not there and they did not know her location. I had a quarter in my pocket, so I decided to attempt to go to the Houston Medical Center, to see what had happened to Donna. I was a street smart kid, who knew how to ride the bus all over the Houston area, as my brother and me would regular catch the bus. I caught the bus route that would go to the Astrodome, as the Medical Center was on that route. I arrived at the Ben Taub Hospital and they had no record of Donna being admitted. There was also no sign of my mother or brother. Not sure what to do and having no money, I began the journey back home to the waterfront. Back in those days hitchhiking was quite normal, so I began to stick my thumb out for rides. The first ride went smoothly and I got about halfway home. The second ride would be just a straight shot down the road we lived on. As we were about 2-3 miles away from my house, the man who picked me up, reached out and touched me on my leg, and I was quite startled. We were going about 20-25 miles an hour as this was happening. Being a scrappy teenager, I immediately swung and hit the man on the right side of his face, and jumped out of the moving car and ran as fast as I could to get away from the car. The man in the car accelerated and took off. As I hit the pavement, I had a few bruises and scratches, and I began the journey home, walking the rest of the way. It was beginning to turn dark, when all of a sudden right near where we lived, I could see my brother and mother talking and they both were crying. They informed me Donna had died. The ambulance did take her to the Ben Taub Hospital but she was dead on arrival, so they did not admit her. Donna had regular bouts of epileptic seizures, as this was the reason why she fell into the space heater. When my brother came home from school he found her and immediately got help to get her to the hospital. At the funeral, I remember the Lord speaking to me in a clear voice, saying *she is with me and she is totally healed.* Thinking back after all these years, I clearly remember the comfort of the Lord in the midst of a cruel day in my life. Jesus truly is the God of all comfort.

*Blessed be God, even the Father of our Lord Jesus Christ, the Father of mercies, and the God of all comfort. **(2 Corinthians 1:3)***

God takes the painful experiences of our lives and helps us to be overcomers in our tribulations and sufferings. Dealing with our pain is very important for us to walk in our God given assignment. Unhealed pain produces unhealthy thought patterns. These pains also produce ungodly beliefs that keep us from hearing what God is saying. Our belief system is not always obvious on the surface. An iceberg is a good metaphor of how our belief systems work. The majority of an iceberg is below the surface and not really seen to the naked eye. Most of what we see on the surface is a fraction of what is really below the surface. The same is true in our thought life. Our subconscious minds can think thoughts that undermine every potential. Trauma and tragic accidents can leave scars in us which need to be healed. When the Bible talks about renewing our minds, this includes both our conscious and sub-conscious mind.

I close this chapter with another personal story of pain in my own life. After I had graduated from seminary in the eighties and pastored my first full time church in Arizona. I experienced a really painful season in my life that was quite overwhelming. I left Arizona and moved back to Ohio and planted a new church. Over 27 years ago after the church had been planted, I experienced a devastating painful divorce. Divorce is a painful experience for all family members involved. In the midst of this very painful season, I visited my old church where I had been an Assistant Pastor before leaving to go to seminary. As I was sitting in the pew during the service, I began to experience quite a bit of sorrow in my heart, as I was remembering the great times in this church with my family from the past. All of a sudden I could hear the Lord speaking to me and saying, *Jack do you understand I not only took your sin on the cross, but I also took your sorrow. Would you like to give your pain to me?* After a time of deep reflection and thought, I went to the altar and I said yes to the Lord and Jesus began to heal my broken heart. When we go through difficult seasons in our lives, it is easy to throw in the towel because of guilt and shame. Many even discourage us from moving forward due to our failures. You must remember, God is the one who directs our lives. God does not throw us away after failure. He picks us up and puts us back together again. If we are always disqualified after failure, then God would have had no one in the Bible that could represent Him, as many of the great men of faith were total failures. Yes you will need major healing from times of failure, but remember God is the God of a second chance.

Are you overwhelmed with sorrow from something that happened in your past? Your pain from the past can either be a stumbling block or a springboard. Which one will you choose? Pain is unavoidable in this life. The key for you, is how will you react to this pain. Do not be fooled into believing you are the only one with this intense pain. Most of the great leaders I know have overcome great suffering and have used these painful experiences to bring life to others. You are not alone. Will you let Jesus heal your broken heart? Let Him come and fill you with His overwhelming love. He wants to use you to touch others with broken hearts. He will use the pain in your life for the benefit of others, so they also can overcome the pain in their lives to fulfill their Godly vision.

Key Question: What one problem would you like to help people solve?

_____

_____

_____

Does your pain motivate you or debilitate you ?

_____

_____

_____

Have you asked God to heal your pain?

_____

_____

_____

Action Item: Identify the one thing you would like to help people to come to understand.

_____

_____

_____

Prophetic Word: _I am the God that healeth thee. There is nothing in your life that I can not heal. Bring your hurts and disappointment to me and I will turn your sadness into a deep joy because you are now an overcomer. You are no longer a victim but a victor. Be of good cheer I have overcome the world._

HELPFUL RESOURCES

Chazown by Craig Groeschel
Healing for Damaged Emotions by David A. Seamonds

Chapter 3
Prayer and Presence the Place of Revelation

Key Scripture: Nehemiah 1: 4 *And it came to pass, when I heard these words, that I sat down and wept and mourned certain days, and **fasted and prayed** before the God of heaven.*

Years ago, I was attending an all night prayer meeting with two other pastors who were attending the same seminary I attended. These two pastors were both married to Korean women who had grown up in a church that had all night prayer meetings every week on Friday nights. These two sisters were use to praying all night on a regular basis and they both had a huge influence on all of us. I was seeking the Lord for the specific assignment and location He wanted for me after graduating from seminary. I had been in prayer for several weeks with no specific leading as I was nearing graduation time with no answer. After about four hours in prayer the Lord clearly spoke to me and said, *tomorrow I will tell you where you are going after you graduate.* I had been preaching in many churches in Missouri and Arkansas, and had several offers to Pastor a church, but I felt those offers were not God's perfect will for me and my family. When we seek the Lord for important decisions in major life directions, it is amazing how he speaks with clarity and precision. The next day, three circumstances clearly revealed the location of my future assignment with a specific city clearly identified.

This is the third time I am coming to you. In the mouth of two or three witnesses shall every word be established. ***(2 Corinthians 13:1)***

In the elevator, in the parking lot and on the phone, God clearly was speaking the location of the city for our next assignment. God wants to reveal His specific purpose for our lives, especially in major situations. When He speaks, it is a great motivational source to know we are walking in His perfect will, versus a plan that we ourselves have devised. When we delight in God, He gives us His desires for our lives.

In an age when church prayer meetings are often a time of asking God to grant all the petitions on our list, we need to understand the essence of true prayer. When we walk in the Kingdom, things we need should not even be on the priority list in our prayer meetings. Jesus promises us He will supply all our needs. This is a promise for every Christian.

My God shall supply all your needs according to his riches in glory by Christ Jesus **(Philippians 4:19)**

The essence of prayer is spending time with God and seeking His heart for our lives. Only two times in the New Testament is the root word for intercession used and it is found in 1 Timothy 2:1 and I Timothy 4:5. The greek word is *enteuxis* and it simply means an interview, a coming together. Our prayer time should be a coming together with the Lord to see what is on His heart. Although there are several other forms of prayer, this form is most important as we are seeking God's heart for our lives. This kind of prayer keeps us from operating in selfish ambition. Graham Cooke in his book, The Newness Advantage, states the following, *"Prayer is about learning to abide in what I have promised and asking in line with My will and desire for you.The best prayer always has a relational base and a functional outcome. In Christ, you are learning to pray with Me, not towards Me."*

Nehemiah knew his next assignment would come from time with the King of Kings, seeking His perfect plan for the next steps in his life. He began to cry out to God asking Him to be attentive with His ears to hear and His eyes open to see the prayer of His servant and the children of Israel also. When we spend time with God, we become quite aware of our own limitations and sinfulness and we begin to ask God for His mercy. Praise God, He is merciful to us and has provided a way of forgiveness and salvation for those who call on His name in Jesus. Nehemiah asked for personal forgiveness and corporate forgiveness for his brethren. When we spend time with God we begin to see how holy He is and He will also gives us a burden for others. Every vision will include a burden for other people the Lord would like to touch. Prayer is the place where we discover our God given purpose and vision.

George Muller, the famous preacher and orphan director of homes for orphans illustrates the power of prayer. He directed orphanages that cared for up to 10,000 orphans. Early on he vowed to God to not ask people for money and depend entirely on God supplying all the needs by prayer. This type of ministry would surely cost a large sum of money and he would believe God for the basic needs of the children. One time in prayer, as he sat with the children at dinner time around the table with no food available, they bowed their heads and prayed and as the prayer ended, someone knocked on the door. It was a baker with fresh bread. Also at the same time the milkman's cart broke down in front of the orphanage, so he supplied them with fresh milk. Prayer is foundational for us to find God's will.

One more story of a discouraged missionary who had been on the field for many years, obeying the call that God had given him years ago. His wife and two children were wondering what would happen the next day as Christmas was coming. The missionary was quite depressed as his ministry had not been very productive and he had seen very little fruit over the years with little to no income coming in from supporters. There was no money available to buy any gifts and he seemed helpless to provide for his family. His daughter was all excited and told her Dad , I think I am getting a doll for Christmas. His son declared he was hoping for a pair of skates, so he could skate in the cold climate they were called to minister in. His wife was sharing how she could sure use a new dress and that it would be great if her husband could at least get a new pair of socks, because the ones he was wearing had holes in them. He went to bed that night quite discouraged, but said a simple prayer asking God to help. Come early Christmas morning, there was a knock on the door and a man had a box to give the family. The tired missionary opened the door and began to slowly open the box before his family had awakened.

Inside the box was a doll for his daughter, a pair of skates for his son, a new dress for his wife and yes a pair of sock with no holes for him. He had experienced the greatness of God supplying his needs supernaturally from a simple desperate prayer. With our God given vision, He will answer the prayer that is according to His will. When we see no natural way for God to work things out, He will provide in unexpected ways to supply the vision He calls us to even if it seems impossible. Remember the greatest part of prayer is simply spending time with our Creator, seeking His heart and His desire for our lives. He has a wonderful plan for your life

And it came to pass in the month Nisan, in the twentieth year of Artaxerxes the king, that wine was before him: and I took up the wine, and gave it to the king. Now I had not been beforetime sad in his presence. (Nehemiah 2:1)

Nehemiah understood that being sad in the presence of the King could be total disaster. He was the King's cupbearer and he needed to represent the King properly, as it would cost him his very life. I'm sure he did not fully understand that the King would actually be a future source for all he would need to fulfill his vision. Likewise, we often do not understand that our heavenly King will provide all we will every need to accomplish His purpose and plan for our lives. As Nehemiah was afraid to be honest and real before King Artaxerxes, we also are sometimes afraid to be honest in the sight of the Lord. We need to come before the presence of the King in humility and honesty.

Thou wilt shew me the path of life: in thy presence is fullness of joy; at thy right hand there are pleasures evermore. (Psalm 16:11)

Do you regularly spend time in God's presence. In God's presence there is *fullness of joy.* Nehemiah got his assignment from being in the presence of the King. John got a revelation of Jesus when he was in the spirit on the Lord's day .

I was in the Spirit on the Lord's day, and heard behind me a great voice, as of a trumpet .(Revelation 1:10)

When we are in the presence of the King, we first get a vision of who He is, then we understand who we are, then we learn what we are to do with our lives. The process in the presence of the King is a vision of who He is, then a vision of who we are. We are to be before we do and then we get a vision of what we do. A revelation of the King, our identity in the King and our assignment from the King. Remember we are in a new season because of the New Covenant. We have moved from a visitation mode to a habitation mode. Quit begging God to come and bring revival, start believing that God has already come in power and He resides in you. Understand we are in a time of habitation not visitation. Jesus will never leave us, He will stand by His word. He will never forsake us no matter what is happening in our lives.

*In whom ye are builded together for an habitation of God through the Spirit. **(Ephesians 2:22)***

Key Question? Do you have a prayer time where you spend time each day with the one who has a perfect plan and purpose for your life?

_____

_____

_____

Ask God specifically for confirmation in His word for your life calling. Write down what He says in your quiet time on a regular basis. Get a journal and keep track of what He says.

_____

_____

_____

Action Item:

Do you have a regular time where you simply spend time with Jesus in His presence, if not start today?

_____

_____

_____

Prophetic Word: *Spending time with me is more important than anything you will ever do for me. As you begin to really see who I am, you will truly discover who you are becoming. You can be like me because I live in you.*

HELPFUL RESOURCES

With Christ in the School of Prayer by Andrew Murray
In His Presence by E. W Kenyon

Chapter 4

Provision an Essential Part of Vision.

Key Scripture: Nehemiah 2: 7-8 *Moreover I said unto the King, If it please the King, let letters be given me to the governors beyond the river, that they may convey me over till I come to Judah; And a letter unto Asaph the keeper of the King's forest, that he may give me timber to make beams for the gates of the palace which appertained to the house, and for the wall of the city, and for the house that I shall enter into. And the King granted me, according to the good hand of God.*

When God gives a vision He will also provide provision for the vision He gives. The good hand of God will supply what we need to accomplish the vision He has placed in our hearts. Nehemiah understood that the King had the resources he would need. God has all the resources of Heaven at His disposal to provide for us all things.

I'm reminded of a personal story in my ministry many years ago to illustrate that provision is an essential part of vision. I was on a hospital call at the VA Medical Center visiting with a man dying of cancer. After a time of prayer and scripture reading with the man, I left to go back to my church office. As I was leaving the parking lot, I heard the Lord's voice say turn left, I want to show you your new house. Struggling with this unusual sense, I obeyed and turned left instead of right, the direction to the highway back to my office at church. Immediately on the right was a big double wide trailer that was opened up and I saw a beautiful fireplace which would be part of the living room inside the trailer. My family had been living in a small one bedroom suite (really a Sunday school class inside the church we were pastoring in Arizona. We knew God had called us to Pastor this church but we needed a place of our own to call home. I pulled in the business and began to look at the house and the salesman approached and told me the price was 22,000$. We had no money and credit would be nearly impossible with an income of one hundred and fifty dollars a week for a family of 6. So I looked at the trailer and told the man, I would pray and see what I could do. As I drove home, I stopped by to see one of our parishioners. As we were talking, the sister asked me a question. Do you know anyone that needs a lot for a trailer as we have one and would like to let someone park their trailer on the lot for free as long as they develop the utilities on the lot? I told them I would get back to them. I left and returned to the church and as I was pulling into the parking lot, an intercessor in our church ran up to me and said Pastor, Pastor, can I talk to you. She began to tell me she had been in prayer and the Lord spoke to her to loan me some money at zero interest. As I heard this, I thought, if the Lord really spoke to her she will know the amount I will need. So I asked the sister how much she could loan me and she stated the exact amount we would need to buy the modular home. At the same time we received an unexpected gift in the mail to cover a 10% down payment. God had surely called us to Pastor this church in Tucson, Arizona, but we had no personal resources to even get a house. God supernaturally provided finances for a house, a plot of land to put the house on, and an interest free loan .

God will supply all we need to fulfill our life long vision. This is simply His Pro-vision.

He is for us, not against us. He wants to provide your every need according to His riches in Christ Jesus. Our King has all the supply we will ever need. God can use many different ways to provide for us. Let me list a few ways he can supply all we need to fulfill His vision.

Your career earnings from you and your spouses job while you work part time on your vision.

Support from others who believe in your ministry such as missionary support.

Multiple streams of income from rentals.

Online income.

Passive and active business income.

Fundraising support from banquet and corporate sponsors from individuals and corporations.

Investment strategies and extra part time work.

Retirement Income.

Inheritance income.

Sometimes in an area such as a church ministry, the parishioners in the church will provide a sufficient income for what is needed. More than one stream will be needed in most cases. Let God direct you in deciding how He will fund what He calls you to accomplish. Sometime those who are in retirement ages, have an ample supply of retirement income to fully fund God's vision. If you are at retirement age, this is the time to step up and let God do the impossible through you. This is no time to sit back in your rocking chair and float off in the sunset. Rise up oh man and woman of God, you are a mighty warrior, with years of refining in the fire of the masters hand. You are indeed ready.

My God shall supply all my needs according to His riches in Christ Jesus. (**Philippians 4:19**)

When Nehemiah came before the King he supplied all that he needed for him to accomplish his assignment. King Artaxerxes provided a letter to the King's forest to provide timber for the walls of the city and the house of God to be rebuilt. When Joseph was sold into slavery, God placed him in Pharoah's house with all the supply he would need to accomplish the dream he had received at the age of 17. When he was in jail, I am sure he thought his dream would not become a reality. His character still needed to be developed so that when he walked in God's purpose for his life he would have a proper perspective and be able to walk in forgiveness toward his family. God was using unusual circumstances to eventually get him to the place where he would have an unlimited supply. This supply would be the source of rescue for his family. Remember God will not only supply what we need, but also supply more than enough for us to help others in their time of need. We must realize God is our unlimited source of all the provision we will ever need. God will supply what He demands. God's grace is His unlimited supply and enablement for us to obey faith. Faith in the Bible comes from us hearing the word of God and God's grace is the power He supplies for us to obey the instructions we hear, so we can be doers of the word.

*For if by one man's offence death reigned by one; much more they which receive abundance of grace and of the gift of righteousness shall reign in life by one, Jesus Christ. **(Romans 5:17)***

Just a word to those who are from the baby boomers generation. We must also remember that timing is quite important in the supply of God. Many times we can go through life not understanding our divine purpose or assignment until we are quite older. We were caught up in achieving success and trying to take care of our families, that often times we spent no time seeking God for our personal vision. Our main focus was on working hard to support our day to day needs for our families. It is not too late to begin to earnestly seek the Lord for His specific vision, because at this stage in our lives we are more financially secure than when we were younger. Many baby boomers have solid resources where they do not need to work and can give attention to purposes and ministries were they can freely give without needing a source of income specifically from their ministry efforts. This frees us up to do unconventional things that most people would never do because they need a strong base of support. Baby boomers also have time freedom that they did not have when they were working 50-70 hours per week. There are many examples of this all around us. If you are between the ages of 55-85 you are a prime candidate for God to use you in unconventional ways where you will not need a steady income each month. Go start a church, head up a short term mission trip at home and abroad. Go back to Bible College or Seminary and get train to be a leader in the church. Go on staff at a church which needs help but can not afford to pay a salary. The opportunities are unlimited.

Let me tell you a story of Harland Sanders, the famous man we have affectionately called Colonel Sanders. He did not became famous until after he was 65 years old. He had a relatively small restaurant and motel in Corbin Kentucky on a local road US 25. When Interstate 75 opened up his business began to suffer and dwindle. Rather than panic and give up, he began to work on perfecting his spice blend and quick- cooking technique. He then began selling Kentucky Fried Chicken franchises and had over 900 location when he sold the business. All this happened after the age of 65.

One of my most favorite TV shows Little House on the Prairie, based on the novels by author Laura Ingalls, were not published until she was 65 years old. Remember Moses had spent 40 years in the desert and probably was over 80 years old when he led the children of Israel out of Egypt. Have you been in the desert? Do you feel you have missed your opportunity to make a difference in this world? No, No, No, you have not missed your time to shine. Rise up oh man or woman of God and let God use your years of experience to minister life to those in need. Open your eyes and look around *the fields are white unto harvest,* with so much need. You might be at that time in your life where all your financial provision is met. Go out and bless someone with the blessing you have been blessed with.

Key Question: Who is your Source? Declare in writing that God will specifically provide what you need.

_____

_____

_____

Action items:

How much money do you need to make per month to live your God given purpose and dream?

_____

_____

_____

Review your revenue sources in your current situation, and identify revenue sources you will need to fulfill your vision.

_____

_____

_____

Do a budget plan of 2 areas; 1.Where you now are financially. 2: Where you would like to be. financially. You can go on my website www.thevisionprinciple.com and download a copy under the tab, resources ; (2 Budget Plan).

After determining how much money you really need to live your God given vision. You will need to eliminate any excessive expenses. Make a list of what you want to eliminate and what time period it will take to accomplish reducing your expenses.

_____

_____

_____

Prophetic word: *I have an abundant supply for all you will ever need.When you walk in my plan for your life, you will always have the provision for the vision. Let me lead you beside still waters, let me restore your soul. Spend time with me and remember I am your inheritance. My supply is unlimited. By your efforts, you can only do so much, but with my supply, you can do all the things I call you to do.Enter into my rest and flow in my river of peace which will never run dry.*

HELPFUL RESOURCES

Transforming Debt into Wealth by John Cummuta
The Newness Advantage by Graham Cooke
Come Away by Beloved by Francis J. Roberts

....

Chapter 5
Passion a matter of the heart.

Key Scripture: Nehemiah 2:12 *And I arose in the night, I and some few men with me; neither told I any man what **God had put in my heart**.*

Nehemiah had passion in his heart, given to him by God. He did not come up with the idea to go to Jerusalem. God had put this assignment in his heart. This was not selfish ambition, but direction from God to know for a certainty of His calling. This God calling gave Nehemiah a private assurance in his relationship with God. What has God put in your heart for your life? The Bible emphasizes the importance of guarding your heart, for out of it are the issues of life.

Keep thy heart with all diligence; for out of it are the issues of life. (Proverbs 4:23)

Your heart is where God speaks to you in a deep way. This is where your passion in God is birthed and flows. The heart is the place of revelation. We must understand that in order to discover your life vision we must know for a certainty where vision comes from. Proverbs 4: 20-23 and Matthew 13:15 talks about hearing with our ears, seeing with our eyes and understanding with our hearts. God's vision comes to our redeemed hearts as He reveals His plans to us. Remember at the Lord's supper one of the apostles leaned on the breast of Jesus. This was the apostle John, who wanted to get so close to Jesus, he could feel and hear His heartbeat. We need to draw so close to Jesus that we can hear His heartbeat. Matthew 13:15 talks about understanding with the heart.

For this people's heart is waxed gross, and their ears are dull of hearing, and their eyes they have closed; lest at any time they should see with their eyes, and hear with their ears, and should understand with their heart, and should be converted, and I would heal them. **(Matthew 13:15)**

Delight thyself also in the Lord; and he will give you the desires of thine heart. **(Psalms 37:4)**

Passion connects you to the why of life. Passion comes from the heart. Passion is one of the ingredients necessary for success. Passion is a key principle of the Kingdom. When we are functioning in the Kingdom of God properly we will function out of a healthy heart. According to Webster, one of the definitions of passion is "an object of desire or deep interest". Desire is an important part of finding our place in the Kingdom of God. Desire is the combination of two words, *de and sire* ,which simply means *of the Father.* Our heavenly Father is the source of our vision. This is why the enemy tries to fill our minds with lies about our heavenly Father based on our experiences with our earthly father. If the enemy can blur our view of God the Father, he can give us false views of our vision. We must find God's heart for our lives. He has good plans. Jeremiah 29:11. He has our best interest at heart. In the best selling author John Eldredge's book, *Wild at Heart*, he talks about the early Church father Ireneaus who stated that *"the glory of God is man fully alive."*

Passion is the heartbeat of God and the ultimate destination of your purpose.The place where you are operating in your God given passion, along with a clear understanding of your purpose will be an unstoppable force in your destiny. Passion from a healthy heart is great motivation. We have a choice to have our hearts serve evil or good. We can choose to serve selfish ambition or choose to serve the Lord in humility. Our redeemed heart is the place we see, perceive and yes even think.

*For as he thinketh in his heart so is he . (**Proverbs 23:7a)**

When we live with our God given passion, we can see and think in our hearts the plans and purposes of God. My heart determines the why of saying something, the why of feeling something and the why of doing something. We can become what we think. The enemy loves to wound our hearts so that our seeing, thinking and doing are all altered. It is vital that you begin to renew your mind each day to the word of God. You must understand what God says about you. He is a good Father and wants you to live a life of real purpose in Him. Godly passion is from Him.

Over the years I knew I had a call to be an entrepreneur, as well as a pastor, teacher, evangelist. But there was a problem. I wanted to learn how to make money so I could teach the body of Christ how to make money. God gives us the the power to get wealth, and I kept seeing all of God's people poor and loaded with debt. I had a desire to help them get out of a poverty mindset and teach them ways they can increase their revenue streams. The problem is the business model and area I picked to work in was not what I had a passion for. When I would start the business, I wanted to make money so I could do what I loved to do but I did not have a passion to just make money. Provision will always follow the vision. The goal is not to make money, the goal should be to do what God has put in your heart. Without passion, when the going gets tough, we will not stick to the calling of God. Vision from your passion will help with developing persistence to stick with the task. Remember passion comes from the heart and not the head. Passion should have a long term orientation, not a short term fly by night focus. Your vision from God will not be a 90 day flash, but a lifetime burden that stays with you year after year.

Let me encourage you to seek out your passion and spend time with God asking Him how you can make a reasonable lifestyle income doing what you love to do. This scenario is the ideal scenario for living God's vision for our lives. When people do what they love to do in God, they seem to have all they will ever need. God will give you wisdom.

What makes You come alive? Can you describe in 30 words or less what you are passionate about in God ?

_____

_____

_____

Can you describe in one sentence, what you are passionate about in God?

_____

_____

_____

If you can only use one word to describe what you are passionate about, what would it be?

_____

_____

_____

Here are 15 questions you can answer to help you discover your passion.

1. My ideal career would be ?

    _____

    _____

2. People seem to compliment me on?

    _____

    _____

3. When I was a child, I would dream of being ?

    _____

    _____

4. When I am with the Lord, I often think about ?

    _____

    _____

5. If I only had one year to live I would?

    _____

    _____

6. If you did not need money I would ?

    _____

    _____

7. When was the last time you felt in the perfect will of God? What were you doing?

    _____

    _____

8. If you could write a book to solve a problem for others, what would it be?

    _____

    _____

9. What are you really good at?

    _____

    _____

10. What brings you the most satisfaction?

_____

_____

11. Who do you admire? Why?

_____

_____

12. What is your favorite section in the bookstore?

_____

_____

13. What make you the most angry about what is happening in the world?

_____

_____

14. What concerns you the most about the issues the next generation is facing?

_____

_____

15. The last time you felt you were in the flow of the spirit and sensing God was using you, what were you doing?

_____

_____

When you have completed these questions, what jumps out. Warning!! If you have a lot of answers that are self centered, you will need to go be with the Lord and ask him why your heart is always set on you and not others. You probably have a weak relationship with Jesus.

Key Question: What do you love to do in God?

_____

_____

_____

Values

Another important principle we need for walking in our vision is to make sure we understand our values. Our values help us to have integrity to pursue your passion. Who you are is important as what you do. Confusion comes into play when our values are in conflict with our passion. As believers we should all have certain values that assist us in making good wholesome life choices.These values act as guidelines to keep us on the right path in our relationship with God and other people. Some examples of values would be the following;

God is first in all decisions; Family is first after God; The Bible is the rule of faith; I will only do what is legal; my decisions will include agreement with my spouse. These are a few examples of values we should hold very important in our decision making process.

Write out a list of at least 7 items that you value. This will help you stay on the right way.

1. _____

2. _____

3. _____

4. _____

5. _____

6. _____

7. _____

You will in no way violate these values as you are discovering, developing and doing your God given vision. You do not want to violate God's Word to fulfill something you are passionate about. If you are required to violate God's word, you have a wrong ungodly passion and need to make changes. Be serious about following your important life values. Neglecting these values can lead to great disasters which can destroy our lives. God might call you to be an entrepreneur and this might require you to be in partnership with someone who is unethical. This is really an easy situation to deal with. Your values tell you that you can not work with someone like this. You will have to discontinue this relationship no matter the cost, as this violates your life values. We can not be people of compromise, even if it cost us everything.

What is the most important value you hold to ? Keep this in the forefront of your mind.

_____

_____

_____

Action Item:

Start today to identify any area in your life that does not fit your core values. Eliminate anything that is contrary to these values. These might be some challenging decisions. Ask God to help.

Prophetic word: *I have placed a seed in your heart that is from me. Spend time with me and water this seed with my love. This seed will grow and become what I desire. Put me first and the Godly desire I have placed inside you will come to pass.*

HELPFUL RESOURCES

The Ransomed Heart by John Eldredge

....

Chapter 6
Procrastinators and problems to overcome.

Key Scripture: Nehemiah 4:10 *And Judah said, The strength of the bearers of the burdens is decayed and there is much rubbish; so that we are not able to build the wall.*

In this passage, rubbish was hindering the workers ability to build the wall. Likewise we too have rubbish in our lives that can hinder us from walking in fulfillment of our God given vision. I call these procrastinators and problems. These are things or people that seem to block the road that God has clearly paved for us to walk on. Do you always find yourself making excuses for not doing what you love to do in God? You are most likely dealing with procrastinators and problems that are affecting your results. It might be a great idea to change how you look at problems. Problems are God's gift to us to show God's promise and provision to fulfill our vision. Problems are also used by God to develop character in our lives. As the children of Israel proceeded to rebuild the wall there was so much rubbish hindering them from completing the task. God's purpose for Nehemiah was to rebuild the wall, yet problems were a hindrance to accomplishing God's vision for his life. God gave Nehemiah the answer to the rubbish so they could continue to accomplish his divine will. Problems are God's gift to us to be overcomers. Problems help us to fulfill God's primary purpose which simply is to be like Jesus. Every problem we encounter will help develop our character to properly display the character of Jesus to those around us.

As we pursue our God given purpose for life, another hindrance will come from what I call procrastinators. These are people in our lives who keep us from progressing in discovering, developing and doing God's will. Many times they will discourage us from pursuing our vision with words, actions or attitudes which seem to immobilize us from moving forward. Crippling words such as "you will never amount to anything", or "you could never do that", or "you are out of your mind". The Bible has a story about this same kind of situation, Joseph the dreamer. Joseph had a dream in Genesis 37 and this dream did not go well with his family. Joseph was born in Jacob's latter years. The Bible declares that Jacob loved Joseph more than his other children. This contributed to his brothers hating him.

And Joseph dreamed a dream, and he told it his brethren: and they hated him yet more.

(Genesis 37:5)

Joseph had a very clear dream from God, but did not use wisdom in when he should share this dream with others. We need to use wisdom when we have a dream from God. Not everyone understands what God is doing in our lives. The word dream comes from the same root word as vision. This dream was definitely a prophetic dream from the Lord about the future of Joseph. Even when our dream or vision is from God, we should be very selective about sharing our dream or vision with others.

Below are seven main areas where you will have problems or procrastinators that will keep you from fulfilling your vision.

1.Family and Friends

Opposition many times comes from those who are closest to us. The enemy uses discord and disunity to distract us from our primary callings and heavenly visions. The following four questions are helpful, for us to sort out family and friend issues. A house divided against itself can not stand. When Caleb entered into the promise land after 40 years in the wilderness, he asked Joshua for his mountain in Joshua 14 and he granted his request and gave him Hebron. This Bible story is quite significant.

Now therefore give me this mountain, whereof the LORD spake in that day; for thou heardest in that day how the Anakims were there, and that the cities were great and fenced: if so be the LORD will be with me, then I will be able to drive them out, as the Lord said. (Joshua 14:12)

The name for the city of Hebron before Caleb took possession was Kirjath Arba. The meaning of this name is the *city of four*. When Caleb took his mountain, the name for the city was changed to Hebron, which means brothers joined. Things were changing from division to unity. Arba was the father of Anak and they were the giants in the land that the children of Israel had to overcome. One of the main strategies the enemy uses is to bring disunity. It is vital we work for unity in our families when possible, as this will hinder our ultimate destiny in God. Below are some questions that might help to bring us in alignment with the purposes of God.

What relationship needs to be healed?

What relationships need to be terminated?

What relationships need to be improved?

What relationships need to be added?

God also desires that we be his disciples. True disciples will have 7 healthy areas in relationships.

7 Healthy Relationships as a Disciple

Discipleship Defined – *A disciple is one who is just like His master and disciplined in all areas of his life.*

1. Jesus had a healthy relationship with the Father. **Matthew 6:9**

2. Jesus had a healthy relationship with the 3. **Matthew 17:1**

3. Jesus had a healthy relationship with the 12. **Luke 9:1**

4. Jesus had a healthy relationship with the 72. **Luke 10:1**

5. Jesus had a healthy relationship with family and friends. **Luke 2:52**

6. Jesus had a healthy relationship with the world. **Luke 19:10**

7. Jesus wants us to have a healthy relationship with our Function, Finances, Fitness and Freedom. **Luke 4:18-19, 1 Timothy 5:6-10, 1 Timothy 4:8, Galatians 5:1.**

For us to be effective disciples, we need to target these seven areas of development. A well rounded disciplined believer will be an effective witness to a world that desperately needs good examples. Does a believer have the following? Circle yes or no and make a note of what you need to work on.

Quality time with God one on one.	*Yes or No*
Accountability with someone of the same sex in a 2 or 3 group.	*Yes or No*
Participation in a small ministry group of 12.	*Yes or No*
Faithful commitment to a congregational group of 72 .	*Yes or No*
Wholesome relationships with family and friends.	*Yes or No*
Intentional Witness to those in the World.	*Yes or No*
Balance in Finances, Function, Freedom and Fitness.	*Yes or No*

Jesus wants us to be whole in our Finances, our Health, our Relationships and our Faith in Jesus.

2. Faith

Faith issues are many times the most important factors in us not fulfilling the vision of God.

Listed below are 5 categories where we can have difficult situations to overcome.

5 categories of Faith issues

- *Sin to overcome Rom 14:23*

- *Spiritual Disciplines Acts 2;46-47*

- *Spoken Words to confirm your call Rom 10.17, 1 Tim. 1;18,2 Cor.13.1*

- *Spoken words to overcome 1 Corinthians 14;10*

- *Scriptural Misconceptions 2 Peter 1:1-4*

Sin to overcome.

Sin is not only the bad things we do, but also includes us not obeying what God has told us to do. Faith as it is used in the Bible has more to do with instructions from God. Faith comes by hearing a word from God. This word is a specific *rhema* word from God that he desires for us to obey. **Romans 14:23** tells us that "whatsoever is not of faith is sin". God gives us a specific *rhema* word and instructs us in His written word and He expects us to obey Him. The good news of God's expectation is that He supplies His grace for us to obey faith. Romans 1:5 tells us the reason for grace is so we will obey faith.

*By whom you have received grace and apostleship, for obedience to the faith among all nations, for his name. (**Romans 1:5**)*

Grace is God's enablement and desire for us to obey faith. What has God spoken to you and you are not obeying? Start today to walk in obedience to what He speaks. What things do you need to stop? What things to you need to add?

Spiritual Disciplines

It goes without saying that each believer with a God given vision needs to walk in obedience and maintain a vibrant relationship with our heavenly Father. We all know we need certain disciplines that we must maintain on a daily, weekly basis, such as bible study, prayer, fellowship, and outreach. Each believer should have an upward, outward, inward and forward focus to our walk with the Lord.

Upward growth in relationship to God. Exalt

Inward growth in relationship to one another. Edify

Outward growth in relationship to the world. Evangelize

Forward growth in multiplication of ministry. Expansion

Spoken words to confirm God's call .

Spoken words over our lives that are sent to us from God will be part of the battle plan we will all use to become overcomers. These words come from 2 sources, other people, or from God directly through His word or the Holy Spirit.

This charge I commit unto thee, son Timothy, according to the prophecies which went before thee, that thou by them mightest war a good warfare. ***1 Timothy 1:18)***

In this scripture Paul is instructing Timothy to wage warfare with the prophecies that were spoken over his life. These words can be road markers that we can look back to so we can confirm the specific call of God in our lives. God uses other people to speak in our lives to confirm what he is calling us to accomplish.

Also God speaks directly to us through his word in Scripture to help lead and guide us. If we are not regularly seeking God and spending time in His word, we will lack a sense of direction. All of our walks of faith should originate from specific words that God speaks to us in his written and spoken word. All faith comes by hearing, and hearing by the word of God.

So then faith cometh by hearing, and hearing by the word of God. ***(Romans 10:17)***

Spoken words to overcome.

There are, it may be, so many kind of voices in the world, and none of them is without signification. ***(1 Corinthians 14:10)***

We all hear many voices which effect what we really believe. I have met many saints who have had words spoken over them, which have totally kept them from walking in their God given purpose. These words constantly play as a recording over and over in their minds, keeping them in torment and bondage. Sometimes these words operate in their subconscious minds keeping them paralyzed. You must hear what God speaks over you. Feel free to go to my website http://theivisionprinciple.com , under the section resources and find the spiritual freedom manual. This manual deals with getting spiritual freedom in all areas of our lives. We need freedom over any words that have been spoken over us from others or ourselves. We must change what we think, what we say, what we perceive, and what we do. We must hear what God and His word say about us. Jesus told us clearly that my sheep hear my voice. A good minister friend of mine preached a sermon on hearing God's voice and handed out a small sheet describing the difference between God's voice and Satan voice

Understanding the Voice of God vs the Voice of Satan

This is another helpful tool to help us deal with our thought life from Rev. Kathy Rankin.

God's Voice	Satan's Voice
Stills me	Rushes me
Leads me	Pushes me
Reassures me	Frightens me
Enlighten me	Confuses me
Encourages me	Discourages me
Comforts me	Worries me
Calms me	Obsesses me
Convicts me	Condemns me

We not only need to understand how God speaks, which comes from understanding the word of God, but we must also understand the voices we have heard from our past that still play in our minds to keep us from being in the perfect will of God. Voices that originated from our family and friends which were not lined up with the word of God. These are lies spoken over us, which keep us from moving forward in our walk with God. Whitney Houston, one of the greatest singers of all time, would always hear voices saying she was never good enough. She always felt she could not measure up, even though she was an incredible talent. We can experience similar voices which undermine what God clearly says about us.Take some time to ask God to help you cancel the effects of spoken words that replay in your subconscious mind which are unhealthy. We can easily develop ungodly beliefs from voices that are unhealthy.

Spiritual Misconceptions

According as his divine power hath given unto us all things that pertain unto life and godliness, through the knowledge of him that hath called us to glory and virtue. (2 Peter 1: 3)

Most of our spiritual misconceptions have to deal with our view of who God is. Your whole approach to life will be based on who you think God is. Is God a tyrant, taskmaster who is angry and judgemental. The key to having His divine power operate in our lives is the knowledge we have about what He is like. You can not understand your on personal identity in Christ, unless you know who He is. We are called to be like Him. Our knowledge of God comes from our understanding of what the word of God says about Him and the revelation in our hearts of what He really is like. In my own personal life, I think my view of God was unhealthy. In my early walk, I thought I had to work really hard to get His approval. I was a performance driven person, working hard to try and please God so He would love me. We do not need to perform for God to love us. We get to perform because He does already love us. His love motivates us to walk with Him, not out of duty but out of love. Over the years, God has revealed His awesome love unto me. I have been set free from an angry God who wants to always punish us to keep us in line. When you experience God's love you will be free indeed. I know God to be the most loving, gentle, kind and trustworthy person ever. His love is not based on our performance. He so *loves the world that he gave.*

Take some time to come up with a realistic list of what you think God is like. Take that list and go to the word and begin to allow Him to transform your beliefs on who He really is in the word. You will be astounded when you spend time in the word and in His presence. Stop, right now and let Him speak to you. Your whole life will change when you began to understand how much He loves you. His love is not based on your performance or behavior. His love is based on your birthright. You have been born into His family. Quit striving to be good, let the one who is good, live in you and through you. You have His very life in you. You can do all things. You do not have some energy, as the new age people say, you have God Almighty who has taken up residence in you. Wow!!! Shout out His Praise!!! We are his Sons and Daughters and Heirs of God with Jesus.

Wherefore thou art no more a servant but a son; and if a son, then an heir of God through Christ.(Galatians 4:7)

3. Freedom

Overcoming freedom issues are major obstacles to God given visions in our lives. These issues which are almost always internal issues, can be quite devastating to us moving forward in our God given purposes. We can be in the right place at the right time and in the right circumstances and still be unable to move toward our purpose because of internal conflict in our hearts. In the ministry as a Pastor and Evangelist, I have met hundreds of people in some great churches, where they keep their wounded hearts a secret from those closest to them. One Sunday my wife Patty and I were attending a service at a great Bible believing church in Michigan. A sister seated in front of us turned around and said, are you Pastor Jack. I immediately said yes. She told us her name and she said I have been a deaconess in this church for 35 years and I am in bondage, can you pray for me. We were in town that weekend to conduct a Freedom Weekend for a small group of believers at a retreat center from several churches, to help them find freedom from their internal hurts. This dear sister had been a faithful leader in this church for 35 years and she was struggling with great internal issues. She was too ashamed to go to the leaders in her church, even though they would have gladly tried to help her, because she was embarrassed to let anyone know she had problems. We invited her to the retreat meetings and she received great deliverance from her issues. Please feel free to contact me at our website www.thevisionprinciple.com and we can come and do a freedom weekend at your church.

Maybe inside you are all tied up in knots. So many believers faithfully attend churches and continue to hide their deep hurts on the inside. These hurts keep them from pressing into the true purposes of God because they feel so unworthy. God wants to heal you, so you can bring healing to others. If you keep ignoring or pushing aside your pains and hurts, you will continue to be in bondage. Jesus wants you free.

If the Son therefore shall make you free, ye shall be free indeed. **(John 8:36)**

Freedom Issues in Four Categories

Strongholds

Satanic Influences

Stinking Thinking

Struggle Flesh and the Spirit

Strongholds

One of the greatest obstacles to overcome as we pursue our God given vision is the influence strongholds have on our lives. A stronghold is a mental fortress in our minds, that keep us in the pits of despair. Stronghold give us a sense of hopelessness that things will never improve. Below is a simple process of a stronghold .

Thoughts - Satanic inspired thoughts are introduce to the mind.

Beliefs - Deep down beliefs ingrained in the spirit of our minds. (subconscious mind)

Emotions- Entertaining these thoughts brings on emotions.

Action- Giving into emotions eventually leads to taking some sort of action.

Habit - Continual participation in this behavior causes us to develop a habit.

Stronghold - Once a habit is developed, a stronghold is built.

For though we walk in the flesh, we do not war after the flesh:For the weapons of our warfare are not carnal, but mighty through God to the pulling down of strong holds;)Casting down imaginations, and every high thing that exalteth itself against the knowledge of God, and bringing into captivity every thought to the obedience of Christ. (2 Corinthians 10:3-5)

On the surface thoughts in our heads (minds) and thought in our hearts are quite different. It is easy to change what we think, but not very easy to change what we believe, (thinking from our hearts.) Strongholds operate more in the area of our hearts and our belief system. When we renew our minds, that renewal must happen both in our minds and in our hearts. Our hearts are changed through revelation from God and his word spoken to us directly. In the New Covenant, God has given us a new heart in the person of Jesus who lives in us now. We need to operate in the mind of Christ, not in our old carnal way of thinking. Strongholds must be dealt with in order for us to proceed to fulfilling God's vision for our life.

Some definitions of stronghold are;

Ed Silvoso- *a spiritual stronghold is a mindset impregnated with the hopelessness that causes us to accept as unchangeable, situations that we know are contrary to the will of God*

Briann Brent & Mike Riches - *a stronghold is made up of sin expressed in a person's thoughts, beliefs, attitudes, philosophies, actions and values that oppose the truth of God.*

Jack Irvin Sr. - *a house of thoughts that are lies repeatedly rehearsed in our minds that are contrary to the known will and word of God that results in repeated actions and attitudes that are unhealthy and damaging to walking in the freedom that Christ has provided in all areas of our lives.*

After your strongholds are dealt with, we will all have to learn how to relate with others whether in our immediate family or friendships, coworkers and associates. If strongholds are influencing you, none of your relationships will work as God has intended.

This Illustration will help us see:

Relationships with Strongholds | **Relationship without Strongholds**

First: Soul

First: Spirit

Second:Body

Second: Soul

Third: Spirit

Third: Body

We must understand we are in a Battle with an enemy who wants to destroy us.

The following scriptures will help is in the battle.

Put on the whole armor of God so that you can take your stand against the devil's schemes." (Ephesians 6:11)

For our struggle is not against flesh and blood but against the rulers, against the authorities, against the powers of this dark world and against the spiritual forces of evil in the heavenly realms . (Ephesians 6:12)

For the weapons of our warfare are not carnal but mighty through God to the pulling down of strongholds. (2 Corinthians 10: 4)

Be self-controlled and alert. Your enemy the devil prowls around like a roaring lion looking for someone to devour. (1 Peter 5:8)

The Spirit clearly says that in the latter times some will abandon the faith and follow deceiving spirits and things taught by demons. (1 Timothy 4:1)

He was given power to make war against the saints and to conquer them. And he was given authority over every tribe. people , language and nation.(Revelation 13:7)

Those who oppose him, The Lord Servant, he must gently instruct, in the hope that God will grant them repentance leading them to a knowledge of the truth, and that they will come to their senses and escape from the trap of the devil, who has taken them captive to do his will. (2 Timothy 2:25-26)

But I am afraid that just as Eve was deceived by the servant's cunning, your minds may somehow be led astray from your sincere and pure devotion to Christ. (2 Corinthians 11:3)

Below is a list of approximately 20 Strongholds.

Divorce	Witchcraft	Antichrist
Rejection	Idolatry	Religiosity
Bitterness	Sexual Impurity	Jealousy
Heaviness	Infirmity	Unbelief
Pride	Shame	Deceit
Rebellion	Control	Stupor
Fear	Passivity	

After you identify any areas of concern, take time to get a prayer partner and pray with them for freedom and deliverance. Understand that you must reinforce your thought life with God's word .

Also spend time in His presence allowing Him to reveal Himself to you and those things His word says about your new identity. Ask God to fill you with the power of His Holy Spirit.

4 main areas in dealing with Strongholds

1. *Ungodly Beliefs about yourself and God*

2. *Demonic Influence*

3. *Emotional Wounding*

4. *Sins of the Fathers*

For more understanding of Strongholds go to www.
thevisionprinciple.com

Satanic Influences

We must remember the difference between strongholds and issues
we experience due to our sin nature. A good example of this is found
in the area of witchcraft. Yes there is a stronghold of witchcraft, but
many times our issues are simply witchcraft operating in us due to
the fact that we are walking in the flesh. The Bible calls the flesh, our
sin nature, the carnal man, the old man or simply the flesh. The flesh
is not referring to our physical body, but our sin nature. Jesus dealt
with our sin nature on the cross and Roman 6 declares *we are dead to
sin, how can we live any longer therein.* We deal with our flesh nature
by denying ourselves, yielding to the power of the Holy Spirit within
us and taking up the cross. We deal with external demonic issues by
resisting them in James 4:7. We deal with internal demonic issues by
casting them out or expelling them.

Nature of Demons

- Persons without bodies.

- Discontented without bodies

Two main objectives

1. To keep you from knowing Christ as Saviour.

2. To keep you from serving Christ effectively.

Understand the difference between the flesh and demonic strongholds.

The flesh is the carcass. The demonic stronghold is the vulture
that settles on the carcass. The flesh must be crucified Gal 5:24.
Demons must be expelled Mark 16:17

Characteristics of the Demonic Influences

1. Entice

2. Harass

3. Torment, Physical, Emotional and Spiritual (the unpardonable sin)

4. Compel

5. Enslave

6. Addictions (includes both Compel and Enslave)

7. Defile

8. Deceive

9. Weaken

10. General Uneasiness.

Areas of Residence

1. Emotions and Attitudes

2. Mind - Doubt, Unbelief ,Confusion, Indecision

3. Tongue- A Lying Spirit

4. Sex- Masturbation, Fornication, Homosexuality

5. Lust - Perverted Desires

6. Occult

7. False Religion

8. All Heresies

9. Physical Bodies

We must understand that we are made up of a body, soul, and a spirit. 1 Thessalonians. 5:23

Before we believe, we operate mostly in our souls and our bodies. When we are saved our spirit is regenerated and we have new life in Jesus. We must learn Christ until He is formed in us. We have been given His righteousness and we learn to yield to Him. We shatter and demolish any stronghold in our lives by the power that works in us. A famous quote by Reverend Bob Hamp illustrates this principle, *freedom is not the absence of the problem but the presence of a person.*

Jesus is the person who is always present in us. He gives us power to destroy strongholds by the power of the Holy Spirit.

Now unto him that is able to do exceeding abundantly above all we ask or think according to the power that worketh in us. **(Ephesians 3:20)**

Stinking Thinking

As we have seen in our understanding of strongholds and satanic influences, we must not leave out the importance our thinking plays on our walk with God and our future destiny. Having prayed for hundreds of people for deliverance, one things remains very clear. We can be free from demonic influence, but we must always deal with daily renewing our minds. Ungodly beliefs are quite detrimental to us fulfilling our God given dreams and visions. Wrong thinking is a reflection of how we perceive things. Our perception is like the lens on our glasses. Once the lens is scratched, we have difficulty seeing properly. When are hearts are wounded we do not see God in His majesty, we do not have a proper view of God.

For as he thinketh in his heart, so is he. **(Proverbs 23:7)**

We must renew our minds daily in the word of God in both our minds and subconscious minds. Just changing your thinking will not necessarily change your behavior. The popular Cognitive Behavior Therapy model that many secular counselors use needs to be enhanced. You must not only change how you think and identify thinking errors, but you must understand your beliefs need to be examined likewise. Our belief system is in our subconscious minds or in our spirits. Do you know how to renew the spirit of your mind. We have all been taught that man is made up of body, soul and spirit and this is true 1 Thessalonians 5:23 . This statement is true but I believe our soul is much more than just our mind, will and our emotions. Our mind is much more complex than just the simple thoughts we think. Experts tell us about the iceberg complex, which describes our thoughts. Just like an iceberg, most of our thoughts are under the surface. Most of an iceberg is not visible to the naked eye. If we only change the surface, we do not really change our behavior. *As a man thinks in his heart, so is he.* We can think with our hearts, which I believe is our spirits. We must not only renew our minds, but the spirit of our mind also which is our hearts. That is why Jesus came and declared He wanted to heal the broken hearted in His mission statement in Luke 4.

The Spirit of the Lord is upon me, because he hath anointed me to preach the Gospel to the poor; he hath sent me to heal the brokenhearted, to preach deliverance to the captives, and recovering of sight to the blind, to set at liberty them that are bruised. **(Luke 4:18)**

Be renewed in the spirit of your mind. **(Ephesians 4:23)**

Our hearts are the deepest part of your mind which needs to be renewed, your heart or your spirit. This is the area where you believe things in your heart that are either true or false. When we receive revelation from God, it comes to our hearts and is the beginning of the formation of Christ in us. Ungodly thoughts take time to change. This happens when we spend time in worship with the Lord. He speak deeply in our spirits to bring healing and restoration. Each day we need to be with Him and let Him speak deeply to us to bring transformation in our lives. Set aside time each day to be with Jesus. Also weekly set aside time to be with others in the Body of Christ. The life of Jesus in each believer will minister to you. Revelation of your God given vision will not come from continual isolation from other members of the Body of Christ. We should have fellowship with God, and fellowship with each other.

Struggle between Flesh and Spirit

The old Cherokee story is a good example of the struggle we face in our lives between the flesh and the spirit. The Cherokee chief was telling his Grandson about a battle that goes on inside people. He said, my son the battle is between the two wolves inside us all. One wolf is evil, angry, envious, jealous, sorrowful, regretful, greedy, arrogant, self pitying, guilty, inferior, dishonest, prideful, superior, and egotistical. The other wolf in this battle is good. He is joyful, peaceful, loving, hopeful, serene, humble, kind, benevolent, empathic, generous, honest, compassionate, and faithful. The grandson thought about it for a moment, and then asked his grandfather, which wolf wins. The Cherokee chief replied, the one you feed.

We must learn to feed our spirit which in turn will help us to overcome our flesh. What you fed grows. Walking in the flesh will keep you from even doing what you want to do. Godly desire is effected by worldly desire. We have a true healthy desire that God puts in our hearts when we are in an intimate relationship with Him. This desire can be corrupted by walking in selfish ambition or fleshly desires.

This I say then, Walk in the Spirit, and ye shall not fulfill the lust of the flesh. For the flesh lusteth against the Spirit, and the Spirit against the flesh: and these are contrary the one to the other:so that ye cannot do the things ye would do. **(Galatians 5:16-17)**

Take time each day to bring each thought captive to the obedience of Christ. Renew your mind to the word of God on a daily basis. Spend quality time with Him so your soul is nourished each day in His glorious presence.

4. Finances

Finances are normally the number one problem or hindrance people encounter trying to live out their God given vision. We either do not have enough money or we have too much debt to be able to transition or develop our God given call. A few examples would be, I am called to preach and I would like to receive training at a college or seminary, but I do not have enough funds.We must remember riches can come and go. We must realize vision keep us thru difficult seasons in our lives when things are not going according to our plans and hopes. Jesus is working all things for our good because we love Him and are called according to His purpose.

JC Penney is a great example of overcoming financial challenges. After much success and accumulating over 1400 stores by the age of 39. Tragedy hit his life as his first wife had died in 1910 and then his second wife died in childbirth in 1923. He also had great losses as the stock market crashed in 1929. J C Penny stock plunged from 120 to 13. He was basically broke by 1932. After these tragedies, he began to sink into deep darkness and ended up dead broke and in a sanitarium. At this time he began to renew his faith and hope, and by the age of 56 he was back on top again. We can have many setbacks, but God will see us through. No matter what you are currently experiencing in your finances, God can get you to where you need to be, to fulfill your life vision.

Dealing with our finances in four areas.

Revenue Streams

Rockefeller Rules

Red monster eliminations

Reckless Spending

Revenue Streams

Our revenue each month is a strong determining factor in what we can pursue in our daily lives. How much money we make can have a tremendous impact on what we can do to move toward fulfilling our destiny, assignment or vision. In addition to our primary jobs or careers, we can increase our income in many simple ways. There are 4 main areas to generate revenue;

Internet, Real Estate, Investing and Business. When you are in the business sector you either work for someone else or you are in business for yourself. Some examples of increasing revenue streams are listed below. Sometimes it is much better if we have multiple streams of income to increase revenue and these streams can be both active and passive income. Active income being trading time for dollars and passive income working for you when you are not actually working but your money is working for you. As the author of *Rich Dad Poor Dad* , Robert Kiyosaki, states in his book, *the greatest investment we can make is developing financial literacy so you understand how to make money.* If you decide to go into business, you may chose to be self-employed or own a business where people work for you. The best business is a business that can be multiplied so that you can receive passive income from the efforts of others. When your income is based on your efforts alone you are limited in how many hours you can work to earn income. Your income is based on your efforts. When you can generate passive income, your income is based on the efforts of others. Online businesses are quite popular and can also generate passive income based on the efforts of others or a system that grows the income level. Below is a list of some simple options to generate more revenue. Your creator lives in you and has given you the ability to create wealth. Seek him for creative strategies.

1. *Check your tax deductions, only pay what is required.*

2. *Start an online e-commerce business*

3. *Work part time.*

4. *Buy rental property with existing investment money.*

5. *Do affiliate marketing.*

6. *Look for a higher paying job.*

7. *Increase your value with more education.*

8. *Stocks, Bonds, Mutual Fund Investing.*

9. *401K, IRA*

10. *Make sure each year you shop your insurance, this can save up to 30%.*

Rockefeller Rules The famous John D. Rockefeller an American oil industry business magnate, received some simple advice from his Dad that started him on the road to great financial success. Rockefeller was considered in his day the wealthiest American of all time.These simple principles were a key to him finding great financial success as an adult. His Dad taught him 3 important rules for his money even as a child. 1. Give 10% to God. 2. Save 10%. 3.

Control the other 80% to the penny. If we all would practice these simple three rules, financial success will be much easier to achieve. Make sure you develop a budget for your finances so you can keep them under control. Make saving 10% an automatic part of your budget, just like you pay a specific bill. Begin to give 10% of your income to your local church where you attend. Almost all financially free people are regular tithers to their favorite charities or places of worship. The importance of tithing helps us to know for a certainty that God is in control of our money.

Red monster eliminations

Debt elimination is critically important for each one of us, in helping to achieve our God given dream or vision. Debt can be an overwhelming obstacle, I call this the red monster. Not only do we need to deal with debt elimination, we must also deal with the root cause of why we are in debt. Debt elimination is not easy if your income is not greater than your expense. You will have to come up with a plan to decrease your expenses with cost cutting measures. Simply track your spending for 90 days. Have your spouse and you write down every expenditure for 90 days. You need to know what areas you are spending money. When my wife and I did this exercise, we were shocked to discover the amount of money we were spending on eating out. We went on a budget and a debt elimination program and we have achieved our goals due to consistent reasonable sacrifice.When you identify your areas of over spending, go on a strict budget that both family members agree on. Take this extra money and accelerate paying on your debt. Take the lowest amount you own first (regardless of interest rate), and pay that amount off. Take the savings from the expense you have decreased and continue to pay off the second lowest amount until it is paid. This is called *debt acceleration.*

List all your debts by the lowest amount first. Example below:

Car payment 860.00 payment 215.00

Credit Card 2405.00 payment 98.00

Student Loan 12000.00 payment 138.00

Pay off the car payment first and then accelerate the 215.00 payment on the second lowest debt.

Repeat this over and over until all your debt is eliminated. Add in any extra money you have saved from cutting expenses and take that money and apply it also to debt elimination. You can do this with not having anymore sources of income. The old saying, you have everything you need in the house. DO NOT CREATE NEW DEBT.

Also take the money you are saving as you are operating in a controlled budget that you will not violate. You can not control what you can not measure. And you can not eliminate debt unless you practice delayed gratification. Take a serious look at why you are overspending. There might be a deep root cause as to why you have wasteful spending. God wants us to be good stewards and not wasteful spenders. Understand that one of the greatest procrastinators in our fulfillment of our God given vision is overspending and a lack of self control in our money issues. Sacrifice now and enjoy the fruit of your labors later. You do not need it all now. Be slow to spend and quick to save.

Before I went off to seminary, we worked hard to eliminate all debt, so we could live on less money for a season. After graduating from Seminary, we took our Church in Tucson Arizona with a huge salary of $150.00 a week for a family of six. We were able to do this because we were debt free. The good news is God blessed us and in a few short months my salary increased 300%. We were able to fulfill the call of God because we were debt free. You can do the same thing with some hard work and sacrifice.

Some simple things you can do to help with debt eliminations are as follow:

Sell any items that you no longer need. Get a part time job. Sacrifice the amount of money you spend on Christmas, vacations and birthdays. Decrease your entertainment spending. Cut off your cable tv. Go through each item of your budget and see where you can cut your expenses. If you can not increase your income, you still can come up with savings so you can eliminate debt. Take all these savings and pay off your debt. There are so many areas you need to consider. Be creative, God will give you wisdom.

Reckless spending

Best selling author David Bach in his book (*The Automatic Millionaire*) calls this the latte factor. This simply is the wasted money we spend each day on a cup of coffee, when we can take that money and turn it into a revenue stream. Wasteful spending is a real hindrance to us fulfilling our God given vision. A small amount of money saved over a period of time can be just the right amount we need to fulfill our vision goals of a new business, a new ministry, or a new career. When you do your financial budget, go through each expense item and see what items you can decrease your spending. Most of the time the entertainment and eating area can easily be out of control. Also remember to check your insurance policies on an annual basis. We were doing a financial freedom class in our church a few years ago and several people saved over 30% per year on their insurance cost, just by going to an independent insurance agent and getting new quotes for the same policies. One brother in the church saved over 300$ per month with this one technique .

If you want more intentional training in your finances go to the link:www.thevisionprinciple.com under resources tab, financial freedom.

5. Fitness

Physical and mental health are necessary for discovering, developing and doing your God given assignment. Experiencing poor health can be one of the greatest procrastinators in our pursuit of our life vision and destiny. Your body can be used for good or evil. Many people believe their bodies belong to them. This is not true if you understand Holy Scripture and apply this to your life.

What? know ye not that your body is the temple of the Holy Ghost which is in you, which ye have of God, and ye are not your own? For ye are bought with a price: therefore glorify God in your body, and in your spirit, which are God's (1 Corinthians 6:19-20)

We are *fearfully and wonderfully made* in His image, and designed to bring glory to Him in our bodies. We should thank the Lord for how He has made us in His image. Our bodies need to be presented unto the Lord as a living sacrifice, holy and acceptable to Him. He has given us our bodies for enjoyment in this life.

*Who richly gives us all things to enjoy. (**1 Timothy 6:19**)*

God gave us our bodies for enjoyment not indulgence. It is so easy to abuse our bodies with things that are quite harmful, both physically and emotionally. When we use our bodies for things outside of God's plan, we will suffer the consequences of our actions. These actions can take a tremendous toll on our lives. Whether we are involved in recreation or work, we need God to guide us along the way. Work was given to man in the garden not as a curse, but as a blessing. Adam was assigned by God to cultivate the garden where God has placed him. We must be willing to work diligently as unto the Lord in all things. We must also understand that excessive, compulsive work, is not what God intended. If our work is compulsive at the expense of our relationships with family, friends and God, our lives are out of balance and submission to the Lord. On the other hand, a lazy person, is not even tired at night, because their bodies are not tired from a hard days work.

*The way of a slothful man is as an hedge of thorns: but the way of the righteous is made plain. (**Proverbs 15:19**)*

Work is a gift from God, given unto us to give us purpose and meaning. Take some time and ask the Lord to help you design a regular exercise plan to keep your body healthy. Also commit to the Lord today, to use your body in the bounds of His perfect will. Get educated on what a healthy diet looks like. Get with your spouse or close friend and eliminate the junk food from your daily routine. Come up with a list of 25 healthy foods and concentrate on those items for your daily menu. This list should include a lot of vegetable and fruits, with a commitment to portion control. Three things I do on a consistent basis, is drink a lot of water, avoid white sugar and walk on a regular basis.

We must also understand that we are made up of three parts, just like God is triune. We have a body, soul, and spirit.

And the very God of peace sanctify you wholly; and I pray God your whole spirit and soul and body be preserved blameless unto the coming of our Lord Jesus. *(1 Thessalonians 5:23)*

Not only should we take time to exercise and maintain a proper diet, we need to take time to develop a healthy soul and spirit. Our soul is made up of our mind, will and emotions. We need to renew our minds, ask God to heal our emotions and surrender our wills to the control of Jesus. What we think about controls what our actions and attitudes will display. The decisions we make affect our very eternal destinies and our daily activities which either bless the Lord or bring Him sadness. Whatever we feed will grow. As a Pastor for these many years, I have seen firsthand, the devastation of believers who have no self-control over their bodies, souls or even their spirits. Our spirit needs to be joined to the Lord's spirit.

Do you have a plan for physical fitness? Write it out.

_____

_____

_____

Are you regularly renewing your mind with the word of God on a daily basis?

_____

_____

_____

Do you have regular healthy times where you expose your self to clean, wholesome activities?

_____

_____

Have you developed a healthy consistent diet?

_____

_____

_____

6.Function

Do you understand the God ordained calling in your life? What about the career you are currently operating in? Do you have a personal commitment to a local church where your serve others with your gifting? Paul understood he was called to the Gentiles. Jesus understood He was called to destroy the works of the devil. You have a specific calling. The Bible calls this our office or function. There are 3 main ares we need to consider; our **career**, our **calling** and our **church**.

Career

Sometimes we operate in a career simply to create an income to pay our bills. This is a needed requirement to support our family needs. Some enjoy a career they absolutely love and it is in essence a true calling from God. In most cases this is not true. It is estimated that over 80% of workers do not enjoy their careers. An important question to ask is, _Why are you doing the work that you do?_ The answer to this question can be quite revealing. Is it for money, is it because of others, is it because that is what my dad did? Ideally the answer to this question should be, because I love doing what I do and I feel God has called me to do this. Many times the opinion of others can control us into doing things we dislike because of their expectations. We must not let others influence our careers. Are you a thermostat or a thermometer? A thermostat controls the environments temperature. If you set the control at 72, the heat will be maintained at that temperature. If you are a thermometer, you simply react to your environment. Are you controlling your environment? Is someone else controlling your environment? Motivational speaker Jim Rohn, tells us we are the product of the 5 people we hang around with the most. Make sure you are spending time with people who are living their passion who understand the calling of God in their lives. You control who you hang around with. Make the right changes and see your motivational temperature rise to new heights. Your career should reflect your calling and be controlled by God's leading and the passion from Him, that He has put inside of you.

There are many career assessment tools available to assist in identifying your career strengths.

Some examples would be Strengths Finder 2.0, and High5Test. You can find these on the internet. I would also recommend the Destiny Finder by Pastor Michael Brodeur.

Another resource is found on my website at www.thevisionprinciple. com under the resource tab, vision assessment tool. You should find it quite helpful. In this book we are helping you find your purpose, passion and power. You need to take time at this stage in your life to invest in making sure of your election and calling. Do not leave this to chance, God wants you to know His vision for your life. There are so many who work a 9-5 job they hate for years, living a life of frustration and fear. Paul knew, he was called to the Gentiles. Jesus knew He was called to destroy the works of the devil, and you should know what God has called you to do. The best of both worlds would be for your career and calling to be the same.

I press toward the mark for the prize of the high calling of God in Christ Jesus. **(Philippians 3:14)**

Calling

For as many members in one body, and all members have not the same office. **(Romans 12: 4)**

The word for office in the King James Version is translated function in other versions. This is simply your practice or work, (praxis) whether it be secular or sacred. In God's eyes, our calling and function in His Kingdom operates everywhere and not just in a church building. So our callings, whether they be in business or the church are all important and valid to God and considered sacred in His eyes. Many have a career based on a skill, but your calling is greater than just a skill, as it includes God's specific purpose for your life. You must understand and be sure to make your *election and calling sure*. God wants you to have **clarity** about your purpose, **confidence** of your potential in Him, **consistency** in the face of opposition, overcoming procrastinators and problems, **creative** with the creator's power He has given you and **certainty** on the passion He has placed inside your heart, **communing** in His presence, **compassion** to others you are willing to help, and **common sense** on what experiences you will use from your past.

There are two aspects to our calling. This is describe in one of Paul's letters to the Corinthians.

Paul, called to be an apostle of Jesus Christ through the will of God, and Sosthenes our brother.(1 Corinthians 1:1)

God is faithful, by whom ye were called unto fellowship of his Son Jesus Christ our Lord,(1 Corinthians 1:9)

There is a specific unique calling for each individual that must be identify. There is a general calling that each believer should experience. Every believer has a call to have fellowship with Jesus. This is the starting point for understanding our vision. Paul's specific call was to be an Apostle. He also understood he was a preacher, and a teacher.

Whereunto I am appointed a preacher, and an apostle, and a teacher of the Gentiles.(2 Timothy 1:11)

Paul had a general call, to be in fellowship with Jesus. We also have a general call to be in fellowship with Jesus. Remember our specific purpose in life is produced out of our personal relationship with Jesus. We must have right priorities in our lives in order to walk in the purposes of God. My personal relationship with Jesus is much more important than anything I will ever do for Him. We need to have an intimate relationship with Jesus. This intimacy with Him will help produce real fruit in our lives, fruit which remains. Paul had his priorities right.

That I may know him, and the power of his resurrection, and the fellowship of his sufferings, being made conformable unto his death. (Philippians 3:10)

Paul did great things in his ministry for God. He also understood that what we do is not as important as who we are in our relationship with Jesus. Our personal fellowship with Jesus is the foundation for all we will ever become. Your specific calling will become clearer each day as you learn to focus on fellowship with Jesus. If you are weak in your fellowship with Jesus, you will be weak in understanding your unique calling.

To discover your calling or vision, you need to understand the following factors:

- Clarity on your Purpose - Why are you here on earth?

- Certainty on your Passion - What do you love to do in God?

- Consistency in overcoming Pain - What problem do you want to solve?

- Compassion for others in Placement and People - Where and Who do you feel called to help?

- Creative with God's Power - What gifts and talents has God given you?

- Common sense on using your Past -What have you experienced that will help you with your vision?

- Communing with God in Prayer and Presence - What has God spoken to you about in the secret place?

To develop and do your calling or vision, you will need the following:

- Partners to help you.

- Procrastinators and Problems to overcome.

- Provisions to fulfill your destiny.

- Process to develop personal character.

- Persistence and patience to not quit midstream.

- Price a commitment no matter what happens.

- Planning to stay on task.

Church

Being planted in a local church or body of believers, is a very necessary ingredient for all of us to discover our God given life vision. We need Godly servant leaders to help guide us to discover our destinies. Real servant leaders help us find our assignment. When we are in proper spiritual alignment, we seem to prosper in finding our God given assignments. When we are in right order, there will be right results. Serving our local church is fundamental to our own personal success. Being under servant leaders makes it easier for us to serve also. As the old song says, *If you want to be great in God's kingdom, learn to be a servant of all*. When you experience your own God given vision, you will most likely have people who are great servants to assist you in your ministry or in the marketplace. You can not expect people to serve with you, if you have not served others yourself. Most great leaders started their training, learning how to serve behind the scenes without any outward recognition. Have you been willing to serve others with out reward? The church should be the training ground for all of us to operate in the Kingdom of God. The church is the place where we should learn how to develop our life in the spirit. The church is not just the building, but our interaction with God's people as we are helping each other grow up unto the head, Christ Jesus. This is a great training ground for all of us to check out our real motives and reasons for serving God. If you do not have a church home, make a commitment today to seek out a place of fellowship where you can serve others.

Even as the Son of man came not to be ministered unto, but to minister, and to give his life a ransom for many. **(Matthew 20:28)**

But he that is greatest among you shall be your servant. **(Matthew 23:11)**

7. Fun

There are 2 aspects of fun which we need to deal with; 1. Do you spend too much time in areas of your hobbies or likes which distract from the more important areas in your life vision. An example of this would be, do you spend too much time watching TV. Delayed gratification is an essential ingredient in experiencing your God given vision. If you always do what you like, you will always stay stuck in a mediocre life. If you live to have fun, your level of deep life satisfaction will be lacking. Take a realistic look at your life and inventory the amount of time you might be wasting with excessive fun or recreation.

The second area of fun we need to discuss, is do you take time to have fun and recreation. Are you a workaholic or a person who never takes time to enjoy life? Are you always isolated from your family and friends, not taking the time to build your closest relationships with the simple pleasures of life? Leisure and relaxation are important ingredients to having a healthy, wholesome life. Jesus even took time to get away from the busyness of life.

And he said unto them, Come ye yourselves apart unto a desert place, and rest awhile: for there were many coming and going, and they had no leisure. (Mark 6:31)

We can easily have two problems when it comes to recreation and leisure. We can have too much or not have enough. Look at this area seriously and decide which part of the pendulum you need to move to. Our options are to decrease our recreation because we are wasting too much valuable time, or we need to begin to take time to have a quiet restful time to refresh and renew our bodies and minds.

Finally the greatest problem or procrastinator in life you will every face is **You**. Understanding who you are and where you come from is vital for living your vision. Our identity in Christ which is born out of our intimacy with Christ is the key factor for us to be all that God created us to be. Understanding your identity in Christ is the key to walking in the image of Christ. We are new creations in Christ. Christ lives in us. Your old nature has been crucified with

Christ. We need to put on the new man everyday. Our sin nature has been dealt with on the cross and should not have dominion over us.

*Let no sin therefore reign in your mortal body, that ye should obey it in the lusts thereof. Neither yield ye your members as instruments of unrighteousness unto sin:but yield yourselves unto God, as those that are alive from the dead, and your members as instruments of righteousness unto God. For sin shall not have dominion over you: for ye are not under law but under grace. (**Romans 6:12-14)***

Our old flesh, our sin nature, or the old man, should not have dominion over us because we are not under law but under grace. It is a great thing to read the scripture above, but what does it really mean, especially the phrase at the end of these verses, *for sin shall not have dominion over you, for you are not under law but grace.* Let me explain. We are no longer under the Old Covenant, which basically says you must do these things and then I will bless you. The essence of the Old Covenant is the word *if.* Under the New Covenant God supplies the if, as in Christ are all the promises of God yea and nay. Grace is the supply for the demand. Under the law, we try hard to serve a taskmaster who is very demanding. We can never live up to those demands because Jesus had to come to fulfill the law of demand. The law simply showed us that we are sinners. Under grace, we simply yield to what God has already done through Jesus. Sin does not need to dominate us because we are yielding unto God. We are now saints because of Jesus. Grace is God's supply and enablement for us to walk in a new law. We are free from the law of sin and death and we now walk under the law of the Spirit of life in Christ Jesus. We are a new creation. We put on the new man which is created in righteousness and true holiness. What a revelation!!! Do you understand this? We are saints!!!! We are holy because He is holy. We are righteous because He is righteous. His power is in us!!!!

*For the law of the Spirit of Life in Christ Jesus hath made me free from the law of sin and death. (**Romans 8:2)***

That ye put off the former conversation the old man, which is corrupt according to the deceitful lusts; And be renewed in the spirit *of your mind; And that ye put on the new man, which is created in righteousness and true holiness. **(Ephesians 4:22-24)***

We have a new identity in Christ Jesus. Below is a list of just a few things we are now identified as in Christ. Renew your mind daily with these declarations.

Our Identity in Christ

WE ARE

Beloved	Healed	Redeemed
Blessed	Humble	Rejoicers
Called	In Christ	Righteous
Comforted	Joint-Heirs	Risen
Complete	Justified	Saints
Conquerors	Longsuffering	Sanctified
Courageous	Loving	Servants
Delivered	Meek	Sons
Encouraged	New Creation	Thankful
Faithful	New Man	Victorious
Forgiven	Obedient	
Gentle	Overcomers	

Make a list of the problems you face and make an action plan on each one you need to overcome.

Every problem comes with a promise from God and His provision. God will provide a way of escape or victory in your situation. Remember when God speaks to us, there also comes the ability and grace to fulfill that word that He has spoken. Included in God's word is the creative power to fulfill His command. What He says He will do. God is faithful to help us fulfill all He commands. God will supply what He demands.

*Faithful is he that calleth you, who also will do it. **(1 Thessalonians 5:24)***

Key Question : What problems do you need to overcome in the Seven areas of Family and Friends, Faith, Freedom, Finances, Fitness, Function, and Fun:

_____

_____

_____

_____

_____

_____

_____

Action Item

Make a decision to be an overcomer. Tamara Lowe, founder of the *Get Motivated Seminars* shares this; "The first step in getting where God called you to go is to decide not to stay where you are."Get a plan to start eliminating all obstacles and excuses and move forward.

_____

_____

_____

_____

Realistically look at those relationships in your life that need to be eliminated. These people constantly speak negative in your life. Those relationships in your life that you can not eliminate, get an action plan from the Lord on how you can improve that relationship.

_____

_____

_____

_____

_____

Prophetic word: *There is nothing too difficult for me. Focus on my power and not your problem. I am able when you are not able. My power is sufficient for you to overcome any situation. Walk in my power and strength.*

HELPFUL RESOURCES

Biblical Healing & Deliverance by Chester & Betsy Kylstra
The War is Over by Andrew Wommack
Freedom is For Such a Time as Now by Vicki White
Automatic Millionaire by David Bach

Chapter 7
Partners to Help with Your Vision.

Key Scripture : Nehemiah 2:12 *And I arose in the night, I and some few men with me.*

In every specific vision God gives each one of us, there will come the need to have partners to help us fulfill the vision. Nehemiah had a few good men with him. True vision will never be accomplished without the help of other people. God has placed us in a body so we can minister to one another. **Vision always benefits other people.** Jesus came to seek and to save the lost. People of selfish ambition use people to accomplish something they want. Vision birthed from our relationship with God edifies and builds people up, and does not destroy or tear down.

There is a business saying that is often used by experts that is quite appropriate at this time. Robert Allen in his book, *One Minute Millionaire*, uses this phrase, a **Dream** with a **Team**, has a **Theme** and can produce a **Stream**. Obviously everything starts with a **Dream** or vision. Then we develop a **Team** to help us. **TEAM** includes the letters **TEAM**, **T**ogether, **E**veryone, **A**chieves, **M**iracles. A **Theme** which describes your vision and a **Stream** to provide for your vision is important for success. We will deal with the stream, later in the book. Ideally, if your vision can be funded with a stream of income, this is the ideal situation. This is important for sustaining the vision. When we work together we can also achieve more. *One can chase a thousand and two can chase ten thousand.*

When developing partners to help with your vision, you need to understand your strengths and weaknesses. You can continue to do those things in areas you are strong and have others help you with areas you are weak. There are several areas you will need to develop partners that can help with your vision. These areas include financial and legal experts, partners for prayer and financial support, mentor or mentors who are doing what God has called you to do, people who speak in your life, and pastoral covering to guide you to your vision, and technical people to help develop your social media and administrative skills. Lone rangers seldom accomplish great things for God. Although this is possible, a team of people who surround us and support us, make the journey so much easier to travel. Jesus had twelve disciples, Paul had many partners that travelled with him and supported his ministry.

We must also remember that we have to be careful who we share our vision with because many will be vision killers. Nehemiah was careful who he shared the vision God had given him. Not all people have our best interest in their heart. Many times this opposition can come from the people closest to us. These people are not the ones you will partner with to achieve your vision, but these people might at a later time benefit from you eventually walking in your God given purpose. Be patient, in time you can surely be a blessings to those who oppose you now. Do not grow bitter or have an unforgiving heart toward them, as they may become your partners later on when the timing is right. God has a way of healing relationship in His time, not our time.

And I arose in the night, I and a few men with me; **neither I told any man what God had put in my heart to do at Jerusalem. (Nehemiah 2:12**

When I was in seminary in Springfield, Missouri in 1985, I met an older couple who were very successful business people who were strong believers. They wanted me to partner with them in a business endeavor, and I gave it serious consideration and eventually decided to not join with them as I understood the vision God had called me to did not include at that time a business.They were very understanding and wanted to continue to encourage me. They told me they wanted to be balcony people for me. They shared a book they had read from Joyce Landorf, entitled *"The Balcony People"* Another way to say this, they wanted to encourage me and cheer me on from the balcony and support my ministry any way they could. Just like this couple who offered to help, we need balcony people as partners who edify and encourage us with help along the way. Lets look at these areas of need, where partners can help us.

Mentor/s

A mentor is a vital ingredient in finding, developing and fulfilling your vision. A mentor is defined in the dictionary as a *"wise and trusted counselor or coach"*. Who is doing what you want to do? Who has been down the road you want to go? This mentor/s can be someone you meet with personally or have contact with through the phone or through the internet. This can include more than one person also. The old Chinese proverb states, a *single conversation across the table with a wise man is worth a month's study of books.* Very few people achieve their vision in life without a personal mentor. Mentors helps us with avoiding key mistakes. Mentors help us develop patience in our journey, because they understand what it takes to get to where you want to go. Mentors can speak into our lives, to motivate us to keep going when things look dismal. If you physically can not meet with a mentor, try to take time to study what they have done and what they are doing in their ministry. Make sure you share the same values with your mentor, as you do not want to achieve success at the expense of violating your convictions about certain areas in your life. What good is it, *if a man gain the whole world yet loses his own soul.* A mentor has skill sets they have developed over a period of time which will help you to avoid critical mistakes that they made on their journey. Make getting a mentor a priority in pursuit of your vision. Mentors are also very helpful to hold us accountable, when it is time to make needed changes. Hopefully you can have mentors who are willing to coach you through the steps of realizing your vision, without the expensive charge that can occur with one on one coaching.

Over 30 Years ago, one of my early mentors, was Dr. Terry Lewis, my Professor of Church Growth at the Assemblies of God Theological Seminary, and the National Church Growth Consultant for the Assemblies of God Church. Dr. Lewis just recently went home to be with the Lord. His inspiration has had a lasting effect on my life even until this day. I spent many hours in personal time with him and began to develop a love for church growth consulting, assisting churches with growth problems. Like Dr. Lewis, take time to get to know your mentor, as there are many valuable lessons they can share with you that is not just information, but useful for personal application. Dr. Lewis had a wealth of knowledge, but one of the greatest things I learned from him was simply to love people. When he would come visit me, he would always invest time with my children, playing *freddy the fork* with them. He cared about people, not just teaching churches how to grow. Try to find a mentor, you can spend time with on a personal level. There will be great benefit to this personal time. As Dr. James Kennedy use to say, *we grow more from what is caught, rather than what is taught.*

Pastoral covering.

Vision very seldom gets discovered or fulfilled for people who are not in healthy pastoral relationship. Joseph dreams never materialize until he was placed with the right people. In my experience those who are in a healthy pastoral relationships, seem to prosper more quickly and smoothly. True spiritual leadership will release you into your life calling, not control you to just fulfill the call of your leader. Much talk in the body of Christ centers around Apostolic and Prophetic ministry being restore to the Body of Christ. I believe this is a valid understanding at this time in the history of the church. But we must understand true Apostolic and Prophetic ministry releases ministry and does not control ministry. Apostolic ministry starts from the bottom up and not the top down.

*And are built upon the the foundation of the apostles and prophets. Jesus Christ himself the chief corner stone. **(Ephesians 2:20)***

These ministries are foundational ministries from which we can build on. We must realize the foundation is on the bottom of the building, not the top. God graciously places true spiritual leaders in our lives such as Pastors or Apostles who help us develop our God given callings. These are equipping ministries to prepare us for our ministry. True Apostles are not people who have a huge network, but those who help set the church in order, starting with helping individuals in the Body of Christ find their rightful place in the Kingdom. Maybe you have not yet found healthy pastoral leadership in your personal life. Be in prayer about this, as strong spiritual leadership in your life will be a great benefit.

To equip the saints for the work of ministry, for building up the body of Christ. **(Ephesians 4:12)**

Seeking advice and counsel from those who are more mature than us, is an essential ingredient for fulfilling our life vision. The Lord has used leaders in His Body to help me discern and discover the Lord's will on numerous occasions. I personally have made many phone calls and visits with pastors and believers who have helped me make vital decisions where I was unsure of what to do. Seek out counsel from Godly leaders who can help keep you on the right path of life.

Every purpose is established by counsel: and with good advice make war. ***(Proverbs 20:18)***

Professional Specialized Experts

You will need to include in your team, professional specialized experts to help you in areas of personal weakness. These experts will assist you in accomplishing tasks which you are not qualified to do. Below are areas you will need to develop a team.

The technical area will most likely be a great need for most of us. In this modern era we need to have a digital presence in our ministry for us to recruit partners to fulfill our visions. This area can include social media, website building and hosting, landing pages, bulk emailers, auto responders, e-commerce for goods and services and online donations. You will need to make a decision on who will be your website developer, who also will be needed to help maintain the website. In the beginning your funds might be limited, so you will need to recruit a volunteer in this area. The more online exposure to your ministry, the more likely you can have partners who are willing to get involved.

The **legal area** will be another area where you will need help. Will you be 501 3C or will you be a not-for profit organization? You will have to get an EIN number, set up a banking checking account, write constitution and by-laws for your organization. When it comes to developing partners for your vision, you can not be a fly by night organization. You need to make things legal according to state and federal laws or you will quickly lose credibility.

The **financial area** will be important to consider in developing partners to help with your vision. The financial system you chose to operate in will be vitally important for partners. What type of accounting system will you use to keep track of partner donations and ministry expenditures? Who will keep track of your charitable donations and yearly giving records? Will you need an accountant to help with your financial structure and tax liabilities? Good financial record keeping will be important for being a ministry or business of integrity. We need to be credible before all our supporters or clients and even avoid the appearance of evil.

Abstain from all appearance of evil. (1 Thessalonians 5:22)

The **family area** is another great consideration for your vision partners. Your immediate family, your spouse and children need to be on the same page for you to proceed and to withstand the opposition you will encounter in your ministry. Your spouse will be the biggest support you will get as you walk down the road of your God given assignment. Both of you being on the same page will be a great blessing or a great curse if there is disagreement. If you are married, it needs to be about us not just you. A divided house will cause great tension in your family, your marriage and your ministry.

Can two walk together, except they be agreed. (Amos 3:3)

The **administrative area** will also need partners to oversee your ministry, whether in a church or marketplace setting. Will you need a board of advisors to help with making financial, administrative and organizational decisions? Do you have someone you are accountable to for your actions? Who will you go to for advice when you are unsure of which direction to take? Will there be a need for counseling and coaching? Finding qualified board members or advisors can be challenging. These partners need to be season leaders who are faithful and trustworthy who have been real servants. Will you have someone who can look at your finances, to give you sound advice when needed? Do not under any circumstance add people to your board who are not servants. I have coached many young spiritual leaders in the Body of Christ and this seems to be a repeated mistake. Do not put novice Christians on your board, especially in the early stages of your ministry.

Prayer warriors

Prayer warriors who support you in intercession and prayer will be needed to bring health and stability to your vision. These prayer warriors should not only cover your vision activity but also your personal lives. Your well being as a person is far more important than just having prayer for your ministry activity. I have been blessed with many people over many years of ministry to have people who really pray for me on a professional and personal level. Not only do they pray for me, but they also are willing to speak to me, if the Lord gives them a word that relates to me. This has been an awesome blessing. A few years ago one of my prayer warriors called me and had a word they felt was from the Lord, that a trap had been set for me, and that I needed to be careful. This word was timely and accurate and helped me navigate through a very difficult situation due to someone I worked with being involved in fraud. God uses other saints to help us along the way, to build us up and to help us with a sense of security that comes from knowing someone is regularly praying for us.

Prophetic Words

Powerful prophetic words can help us with our vision, given by reputable Christians who are gifted in speaking life into those they pray for. Prophetic words given help to confirm your call. God gives the vision and others will confirm what God has already spoken in your heart. God uses credible people to speak into our lives to encourage us along the way. Many years ago, I attended a conference in Pittsburg, Pennsylvania and the speaker was Dr. Edwin Louis Cole, founder of the Christian Men's Network. There were about 2,000 people in the audience, and as Dr. Cole was speaking he stopped in the middle of his sermon and pointed up in my direction and looked right directly at me and said, young man you are really struggling on the inside about whether or not God is calling you. You are going back and forth, saying in your mind, is this God or is this me. He very forcefully said, "it definitely is God. " This was exactly what was happening in my life. I was quite unsure whether God was calling me to preach or whether I was calling myself. After this word by Dr. Cole, I was quite convinced of the calling God had on my life to be a preacher. This word and many other words from Scripture and other credible saints, helped to confirm God's vision for my life. God will bring you confirmation to the call on your life through other people. When we have God's word, prophetic words and the witness of the Holy Spirit inside us, we can move forward with assurance we are headed in the right direction. If you do not have confirmation, please be slow to push forward, as there *is safety in a multitude of counselors.*

This charge I commit unto thee, son Timothy, according to the prophecies which went before thee, that thou by them mightest war a good warfare. (1 Timothy 1.18)

The greatest partner

The greatest partner we will ever have is God. God works with us and in us to accomplish His will in our lives. The God of the universe lives inside of you. You might feel inadequate, but God is totally up for the task. He can move mountains, create something out of nothing, simply speak and things come into being. There is no partner like Jesus. Those who are self-help experts are missing the most important ingredient in a partner. God!!!! Throughout Holy Scripture God continually works with man to accomplish great purposes. He wants us to help Him display His Kingdom to a lost and dying world that desperately needs to be redeemed. In the famous Lord's prayer we all have prayed on many occasions, there is a profound phrase, "Thy Kingdom come on earth as it is in Heaven." Jesus has us praying for heaven to come to earth. I believe He already started bringing heaven to earth with the incarnation of Jesus Christ the Son of God. Immanuel, God is with us. Our main goal as believers is to display the character and rule of the King. When people see us they see Jesus because we are like Him, conformed to His image.

Therefore the Lord himself shall give you a sign; Behold, a virgin shall conceive, and bear a son, and shall call his name Immanuel. (Isaiah 7:14)

Key Questions: Have you begun to put together your team ? Write down which areas you already have help based on the above categories:

Mentor/s _____

Pastoral Covering _____

Professional Experts:

Legal _____

Financial _____

Administrative _____

Financial _____

Family _____

Write down which areas you need help.

_____

_____

_____

_____

Action Item

Contact your current partners and thank them for their support. Also ask them if you can be accountable to them as they help you stay on task. Also contact potential new partners that you will need and begin to develop a relationship with them

Prophetic word: *Open your eyes and see the people I have placed in your life. Do not run away from those who would correct you, as I have placed them in your life, not to control you but to release you*

into my purpose. Ask me for help and I will send those who you will need to partner with for you to fulfill my plans.

HELPFUL RESOURCES

Team Ministry by Dick Iverson
The Beginner's Guide to The Gift of Prophecy by Jack Deere

Chapter 8
Process to develop character

Key Scripture:Nehemiah 6:13 *So the wall was finished in the twenty and fifth day of the month Elul, in fifty two days.*

Every vision will include process. It took 52 days to rebuild the wall but years of planning and preparation. The refinement of Nehemiah's character took years. Moses was on the back side of the desert for 40 years as God got him ready to be the deliverer of the children of Israel in bondage to the Egyptians. Joseph took years before he was positioned by God to be in charge of the storehouses of Egypt to help provide for his family in an incredible time of famine. Paul had fourteen years in the desert before he was ready to preach the unsearchable riches of Jesus as he needed deep revelation before he began his ministry. Jesus was 30 years old before He began his 3-1/2 year ministry on earth. My own journey of finding and fulfilling my God ordained vision required years of training and preparation. The myth of overnight success can easily mislead us unto frustration and despair. Process is absolutely essential for long term success, which in the Christian world involves obedience. Personal vision will include a definite process that none of us can shortcut. Generally speaking most of us will have a long process to ultimately experience our God given vision. We must understand there is a difference between going in circles versus going in cycles. When we are not clear on our vision, we easily can travel in circles. We seem to move but it feels like we are traveling in a circle. This is a picture of a mind that has not been enlightened. Clarity will come at the right time, when we are in right relationship with the Lord and His timing is crystal clear. Also seasons in life change, which will dictate a different response because of the season. Your calling might be quite different in your 20's versus in your 60's. The process will definitely be different depending on the time that God uses to develop character. As we mature and age, our calling can change quite quickly.

There are 4 areas we need to consider in the process of vision. I call these four areas the 4 D's.

Stage 1. **D**iscovering the Vision;

Stage 2. **D**eveloping Character and Skill for the Vision;

Stage 3. **D**ealing with the Death and Re-birth of the Vision;

Stage 4. **D**efining and Doing the Vision.

1. Discovering Your Vision

Discovering your vision will involve a time process to discern if this vision is a true vision or a false vision. Many things will manifest in our lives that will distract us from our ultimate calling.

This area can seem somewhat difficult because many do not have a clue about their heavenly vision. In ministering in all types of churches with different denominations, cultures and socio- economic backgrounds, I would safely say that over 80-90 percent of believers do not have a heavenly vision for their lives. The good news is that if you are earnestly beginning to seek your heavenly calling, you are on the right path of acceleration, as God will reward those who diligently seek him. He wants you to know your steps are ordered. It is hard to come up with an all inclusive formula for all situations to discover your God given vision, but understanding and identifying the following areas will help:

Purpose + Passion + Place/People + Pain + Power + Prayer/Presence + Past Experiences

All of these factors put together will bring some real clarity to discovering your vision. Most of these areas have been dealt with in a previous chapter. For more detail and help with these areas go to our website www.thevisionprinciple.com under the resources tab and use the vision assessment tool.

2. Developing Character and Skill for the Vision

Knowing your vision is one thing, developing character and the skill to fulfill your vision is another situation entirely. When Joseph received his dream, he had very little character and wisdom in his life to fulfill that dream. God had to take him on a journey, to begin to refine him, so he could ultimately fulfill his destiny. His brothers meant it for evil, but God took those awful events to produce a deep character in Joseph. In a powerful scene, during the time when Joseph and his brothers were returning to Egypt after burying their Father in Canaan in the cave that Abraham had bought in the field of Machpelah, they were all gathered alone to deal with a situation from years ago when they had sold him into slavery. Joseph reveals the heart of God in this meeting with the power of forgiveness.

And Joseph said unto them, Fear not: for I am in the place of God? But as for you, ye thought evil against me; but God meant it unto good, to bring to pass, as it is this day, to save much people alive. (Genesis 50:19-20)

He was sent ahead on an important assignment, so that he could actually rescue his family members, who wanted his destruction. God is still doing the same thing in our lives. Have you been deeply mistreated by family members and friends? Perhaps they have done unspeakable things to you in your past? Have you been a victim of abuse or neglect? Just like Joseph, God is sending you ahead on an assignment to bring rescuing life to those who hurt you the most. What part of this process are you currently in? Those hurts and disappointments are actually divine appointments for your future assignment. You will need, with God's help to deal with these issues, because God wants to display His power in you to reveal His love to those who have hurt you. You will not be able to escape this process. Just like Joseph needed to be in the pit and prison so he could develop character for his future, we also will have our own situations to overcome. God takes the painful events of our lives, so that eventually we can minister His life to others. This will be part of our story and message as God gives us our message out of our mess. God is not in a hurry. He will develop our character to help us become like Jesus. This is God's main purpose on the earth.

Now therefore be not grieved, nor angry with yourselves, that ye sold me hither:for God did send me before you to preserve life. **(Genesis 45:5)**

God is in the rescue business, to rescue those who do not deserve His mercy and kindness.

Joseph brothers were not deserving of mercy, but neither are we. And we must remember that Joseph brought all this upon himself because in Genesis Chapter 37:1-2 the Scriptures declare that Joseph brought an evil report about his brothers to his father. This started the hatred his brothers had towards him. None of us are innocent in the sight of God. We all need the mercy of God in our lives. Take some time to share those hurts with the Lord right now. He is the one who heals and delivers and make us whole. Lord Jesus touch your servants today. The definition of salvation, *sodzo,* is not just a trip to heaven, but an encounter with Jesus who makes us whole.

3. Dealing with the Death and Re-Birth of the Vision

When walking down the journey of life that Gods has ordained for each one of us, we will encounter some drastic experiences that are unavoidable. I am sure there might be some exceptions to this rule, but people seem to go through a specific cycle of life. Dr Bill Gothard, *founder of the Institute in Basic Life Principles*, would teach that there was a clear cycle to all of our visions. This cycle would include the Birth of a Vision, the Death of a Vision, and the Rebirth of a Vision.

Maybe you have been thru this cycle in your own life. I can say with a certainty, that I have experienced this very cycle in my own life. I can remember the great excitement when I began to understand with clarity my personal heavenly vision from the Lord, that I would be a preacher. The birth of my vision was such an exciting time, as I knew beyond a shadow of doubt the Lord's calling in my life. Once I discovered this vision, I began to make a specific plan of execution to carry out this call. I was doing anything I could to get ready to leap into action. I received all the training academically and practically. The Lord open doors of great opportunity for me to preach, teach and counsel on a regular basis to help in my personal development. I then felt I needed more intensive training to attend seminary, as I felt I still was not totally qualified. My denomination did not require a Masters degree, but I personally felt I needed the training. After several years of hard work and sacrifice, I began to live my dream of being a Pastor of a church. I was willing to pay any price and I moved 2,000 miles across the country to fulfill God's plan. I can remember sitting in my church office, thinking, wow I am living my God given dream at the age of 33. Little did I know that my future would hold some incredible difficult things that would shake the very foundation of my vision. I was soon to experience the painful process of a divorce and the beginning of going thru the stage of the death of my vision. This might not always be true for all of us, but there seems to be a pattern in most of our lives that indicates we will go through this part of the process. I not only began to experience this stage, but I had reputable people tell me I was finished. There were days I felt this very thing, I am finished. I will never recover from the death of this vision. Maybe at this stage of your life, you can relate to what I am saying. Did you at one time burn with fire and passion and walk in the clear concise will of your God given dream? There is no better feeling than when we are walking in what we call the perfect will of God. This time in our lives is so invigorating and joyful. We would love for this stage to last forever, but many times it does not. At this stage in our development, we must understand that God wants to take us deeper and closer to Him. Sometimes our journeys have been way too easy, and our inner life is lacking and our relationship with God has easily become mundane. As we have seen earlier, we need time to develop character and skill to properly perform our call for the long term, knowing our relationship with God is most important, not what we do for God in our ministries. In my own life and in the lives of others, I have seen great gifting with swallow character. People can have a great anointing, but do not have the reputable character of a righteous life. Are you a person who has great gifting, but your personal life is a disaster? God wants all of our lives to reflect the character of Jesus. He wants us to be rightly related to Him and to others. When we are in Christ we are being conformed to His image. We have been given a new identity so others can see Jesus in us. We need development in our identity in Christ, as well as clarity on what we do for Christ.

The good news is, this part of the process does not stop at the death of the vision stage, but moves into the rebirth of the vision stage. God is the God of the second chance. People around us might give up on us, but God who is rich in mercy, will not give up on us. A popular song from the 80's by the Hemphill's, *He's still working on me, to make we what I need to be. It took him just a week to make the moon and stars. The sun and the earth and Jupiter and Mars. How loving and patient, He must be, cause He's still working on me.* The rebirth of the vision stage is enjoyable to those experiencing the turn of events and the hope of new life, kind of like a new resurrection. When we have been given up for dead, God specializes in bringing us back to life. He brings *beauty out of ashes.* God is not finished with you yet.

This season of the rebirth of our vision, brings great adjustment and correction in our lives, so that we can be more fruitful and bear much more fruit. God specializes in pruning the things in our lives that are not connected to His supply of life. Some things initiated in self effort can be good, but are not the best that God has for us.

Every branch in me that beareth not fruit he taketh away: and every branch that beareth fruit he purgeth it, that it may bring forth more fruit. *(John 15:2)*

4. Defining and Doing the Vision

After going through the process of the death and rebirth of our vision, we often times experience a real refining of what we hold to be true. We begin to step out and take action to walk in our God given vision. We have come to understand that we must have marching orders from the Lord, and His power supply to maintain the discipline we will need to not quit.

For ye have need of patience that after you have done the will of God, ye might receive the promise.(Hebrews10:36)

We must remember that as long as we are in this life, we will be in process. On this side of glory we are not a finished product. Jesus is conforming us to His image, using anything He sees fit to accomplish His main purpose in our lives, which is simply helping us to become like Him. This makes it abundantly clear that we all need a Saviour each and every day because of our imperfections and faults. As God begins to rebuild your personal vision, understand that this is a new day. The sky is the limit. Do not let regret paralyze you to keep you from starting all over in pursuit of God's amazing plan for your life. Get around others who have also been overcomers. I think you will be quite surprised to learn about many who are successful, who have gone through terrible events in their lives and started over again. Many people might remind you about your failures, but God will use your failures to touch others with His awesome merciful power. Make sure you take the time to invest in yourself. If you will do the work to discover, develop and define your God vision, your chances of success are far greater.

*Being confident of this very thing, that he which hath begun a good work will perform it until the day of Jesus Christ. **(Philippians 1:6)***

Key Question: What stage of the process of your vision do you think you are currently experiencing?

_____

_____

_____

Action item: No matter what stage of the process you are currently experiencing, the most important thing you can do is draw close to the Lord. Deepen your relationship with Him. Just spend time being with Him daily.

Prophetic word: *I am more concerned with what I am doing in you, before what I will do through you. Quit striving to be good and know that I am good. Let my goodness lead your life. Be kind to others as I am kind to you.*

HELPFUL RESOURCES

Extraordinary by John Bevere

Chapter 9
Power will be supplied.

Key scripture : Acts 1:8 *But ye shall receive power, after that the Holy Ghost is come upon you: and ye shall be witnesses unto me both in Jerusalem, and in all Judea, and in Samaria, and unto the uttermost part of the earth.*

Do you have the **Power**? You shall receive power after the Holy Spirit comes upon you. Your power is the gifting that God gives you. For whatever God calls you to participate in He will give His power to accomplish His mission. God is omnipotent, all powerful. His power is in us. When we are born again, we received an inheritance in Christ as Sons and Daughters. We are joint heirs with Christ. When we identify the power we have received from God, we can begin to understand what God is calling us to do. We receive power and authority from Christ to do what He has assigned us to do. In Christ we have all we will ever need and all the authority to accomplish His purpose in our lives.

*Faithful is he who calleth you, who also will do it. **(1 Thessalonians 5:24)***

Many years ago when I was a freshman in college, I had to give a speech for a communication class. At that time I was extremely nervous and totally afraid to speak in front of people in any manner. The Professor let me pick any topic for the speech and use any aid if necessary to help with the presentation. I chose to talk on how to dribble a basketball. The reason I chose this topic was I had much nervous energy and needed something to calm me down. The whole time I talked, I dribbled a basketball. My communication skills were very weak. During this time I was beginning to understand that God was calling me to preach and I was as Paul said *"in fear and much trembling"*. My first sermon was just a year later as I preached in front of a packed church doing what God had called me to do. In my natural ability, I was extremely fearful and intimidated. Much to my surprise, the sermon was very effective as almost the whole church came forward to receive Jesus. God has given us His power to do supernaturally *above all we can ask or think according to the power that works in us*. In our weakness, He is strong. In our fears, He is love. In our nervousness, He is our peace.

And he said unto me, My grace is sufficient for thee: for my strength is made perfect in weakness. Most gladly therefore will I rather glory in my infirmities, that the power of Christ may rest upon me. (2 Corinthians 12:9)

He has given us His power so we can be like Jesus and do what Jesus did. We have the power of the Lord. In our weakness He is strong. When we walk in the Spirit we have access to His ability and power. God's gifts are supernatural and spiritual gifts that He has made available to us by the power of the Holy Spirit. The Spirit of God will gives us what we need when we need it. His timing is perfect and complete. Inherent in God's gifting is the ability to fulfill and supply all that He demands. Understanding the power of the New Covenant, we must understand what God demands, He supplies through His abundant grace.

For if by one man's offence death reigned by one; much more they which receive abundance of grace and of the gift of righteousness shall reign in life by one, Jesus Christ. (Romans 5:17)

God wants us to reign in this life and be overcomers and more than conquerors through Him. Many have defined grace as undeserved favor, but I think this popular definition is lacking. Grace is God's enablement and power for you to obey faith. He gives us His power so we can do through Christ what we can not do by our own strength and power. **So many people complain about those who preach grace are giving people a license to sin, no,no,no, it is just the opposite, grace is the power God gives us to not sin. Praise the Lord!!!!!**

God's power includes 3 main areas in our lives.

1. Spiritual Gifts.

2. Natural Talents and Abilities.

3. Past Experiences and Skills.

1. Spiritual Gifts.

There are 3 main areas for God's spiritual gifts.1. Ministry Gifts, 2. Motivational Gifts and 3. Manifestation Gifts.

Ministry Gifts would include Pastor, Teacher, Evangelist, Prophet and Apostle. These are equipping gifts to help the body of Christ grow to maturity in Christ and to develop the ministry that Christ has called us to function in. As we have shared earlier, each person has a function in Christ or an office in Christ. As we have a function given by Jesus, he uses these ministry gifts to help develop us for healthy ministry. "Iron sharpens iron." These ministry gifts are listed in Ephesians 4:11. Your personal vision might include a call to one of these 5 areas. Over a period of time your call might change to a different role, due to your maturity or seasons in your life. These are leadership gifts to oversee the body of Christ. You might do evangelism, but that will not necessarily mean you are a five-fold minister. You will know you are a five-fold minister when other leaders in the body of Christ recognize your gifting. Do not raise yourself up, let Jesus and others raise you up.

Motivational Gifts would include areas listed below:

Hospitality - (Romans 12:13)

Giving - (Romans 12:8)

Intercessory Prayer - (Colossians 1:9-12)

Mercy - (Acts 16:33-34)

Administration - (1 Corinthians 12:28)

Exhortation - (Acts 14:22)

Leadership - (1 Corinthians 12:9)

Singleness - (1 Corinthians 7:7-8)

Prophecy - (Romans 12:6)

Helps - (Romans 16:1-2)

Music - (1 Chronicles 16:41-42)

Teaching - (Acts 20:20-21)

Exorcism - (Acts 16:16-18)

Craftmanship - (2 Chronicles 34:9-13)

Service - (Galatians 6:10)

Missionary - (Acts 13:2-3)

These motivational gifts will assist you in finding and fulfilling your vision. What God calls you to do, He will give you gifts to fulfill that call.

Manifestation Gifts would include the 9 gifts of the Spirit listed in 1 Corinthians 12. These gifts include the word of wisdom, the word of knowledge, faith, gifts of healings, working of miracles, prophecy, discerning of spirits, divers kinds of tongues, and interpretation of tongues. These are gifts that are manifested when needed through the body of Christ as the Holy Spirit directs. These are supernatural gifts that God manifests to profit all around. These gifts help people, not harm them. They need to be operated in love and with pure motives for the benefit of other people. The gifts we have been given and the gifts we operate in, are an indication of what God is calling us to fulfill. It is important we know how we are gifted to identify an important component in our discovery of our vision. God uses the gifts of the spirit in our lives and the lives of others to assist in building us up to be equipped to find and fulfill or heavenly vision. There are many spiritual gifts test available, to help us identify these gifts. Ask your local Pastor for help in this area. You can also go to my website www.thevisionprinciple.com under the resources tab and use the vision assessment tool for this purpose.

Included in power is the potential God gives us to achieve what He calls us to do. When God gifts you, it is an indication of what He is calling you to accomplish. If you are called into ministry, what ministry, and motivational gifts has He given you? He will use the manifestation gifts in you when the situation requires these gifts. These manifestation gifts do not always operate has often as the ministry gift or motivational gifts, but they are available when needed. God will equip you with gifts that will fulfill your calling. Also God will use five- fold ministry gifts to help equip you for works of service.

To summarize this section on power being supplied, the greatest power of all is that we have been given an inheritance which is priceless. Our inheritance is "Christ in us the hope of Glory". We can do all things through Christ. His unlimited power is working in us to accomplish His will and purpose in our lives, conforming us to the image of Jesus. As Jesus was in the world, scripture says we are also. 1 John 4:17. Cast off the w*ow is me mentality* and put on Jesus , *who is your life.* His power is working in us so that we can do whatever He calls us to do.

Now unto him that is able to do exceeding abundantly above all that we ask or think, according to the power that worketh in us. **(Ephesians 3:20)**

We must understand the power of the New Man in Christ Jesus. I might surprise you with this statement and it could also offend you, but God is not trying to make you better. For years I struggled with taking time as a Pastor to counsel people. I could not put my finger on what it was that made me uneasy. I would spend hours talking to the saints trying to help them improve their lives and help them with their problems. I did not fully understand the New Covenant as God had to come to my heart and give me fresh revelation of what happened with the New Covenant. God does not want to improve your old man, He crucified your old man. Improvement is not His plan. His plan is the New Man created in righteousness and holiness. God is primarily not dealing with your behavior but helping you see your new identity in Christ. You are a new creation learning how to be the image of Jesus. Your old sin nature has been dealt with. You can not improve the old man, he is dead. We need to walk in newness of life in the power of the new man in Christ. We have the God of the universe living inside of us. Your behavior now is birthed in your new identity. Because God lives in you, then you can become like Him and do the things that He does. This is a revelation that will set you free from trying to perform to gain His love. We get to perform because of His love. Our behavior changes because of our new birthright in Jesus, not because of our great efforts. THANK YOU JESUS. Put off the old and put on the new man.

That ye put off concerning the former conversation the old man, which is corrupt according to deceitful lusts; And be renewed in the spirit of your mind; And that ye put on the new man, which after God is created in righteousness and true holiness. **(Ephesians 4:22-24)**

2. Natural Gifts

God has also gifted us with natural abilities which are still given to us by God but they are not necessarily supernatural gifts. These abilities enable us to be good at something. Here is a list of some natural abilities that you might possess or have been developing. Circle at least 5 abilities you think you actually possess.

Entertaining ability: to perform, act, dance, speak, sing.

Recruiting ability : to enlist and motivate people to get involved.

Interviewing ability: to discover what others are actually like.

Researching ability: to read, gather information and collect data.

Artistic ability : to conceptualize, picture, draw, paint, photograph, or make renderings.

Graphics ability : to lay out, design, create visual displays or banners.

Evaluating ability : to analyze data and draw conclusions.

Planning ability: to strategize, design and organize programs and events.

Managing ability: to supervise people to accomplish a task and coordinate the details.

Counseling ability: to listen, encourage and guide with sensitivity.

Teaching ability: to explain, train, demonstrate, tutor.

Writing ability: to write articles, letters, books and blogs.

Editing ability: to proofread or rewrite.

Promoting ability: to advertise or promote events and activities.

Repairing ability: to fix, restore, maintain.

Feeding ability: to create meals for large or small groups.

Recall ability: to remember or recall names and faces.

Mechanical operating ability: to operate equipment, tools and machinery.

Resourceful ability: to search out and find inexpensive materials or resources needed.

Counting ability: to work with numbers, data or money.

Public relations ability: to handle complaints, and unhappy customers with care.

Welcoming ability: to convey warmth, develop rapport, making others feel comfortable.

Composing ability: to write music and lyrics.

Landscaping ability: to do gardening and work with plants creatively.

Decorating ability: to beautify a setting for a special event.

Other not listed:

_____

This list is not meant to be exhaustive. You might have an ability that you are certain you possess. Write it down in the other not listed area as a reference. When God calls you, it will become abundantly clear what abilities you have, that God will use. Not to long ago I made a decision to not work full time and devote more time to my church. So I took a huge cut in pay and went to part time status with another company. I had been working in the manufacturing area and had made good money. I took a part time job with a website development and hosting company and learned some skills that I currently need in my ministry to help others. I do personal coaching and consulting with individuals and churches to help them find and develop their visions. God is using the training I received with that website hosting company for the benefit of others. Make sure you identify areas of abilities you have experienced, this will help you see the hand of God in using your talents for his glory.

3.Past experiences and skills

These experiences are powerful lessons we can use for God to fine tune our personal visions. What have you been doing in your life that you can use to help pursue your passion? Sometimes the Lord has us go on detours, using things which do not make sense that we are doing or have done, to later use these experiences to enhance our God vision. God has shaped your past experiences to develop you for your future destiny. He has masterfully used your past experiences to equip you for heavenly purpose and vision. Your past history is useful for his- story in the future and also in your present. *Graham Cooke*, speaker and founder of Brilliant Book House, speaks of Christians being *present future*. We can not live in the past, but we can learn from our past. Make an inventory of things you have done in past jobs. Think of any skills you used and had to learn or develop for your jobs. Take a look at this inventory and see if there is any patterns that is developing. God will use these skills to help you fulfill your vision. These skills were not just random developments, but God ordained experiences that He knew you would need sometime in the future.

And we know that all things work together for good to them that love God, to them who are called according to his purpose. **(Romans 8:28)**

Make a list of skills you have used in the past jobs.

_____

_____

_____

_____

_____

_____

_____

Skills to be acquired and to be improved

Make sure you are willing to take an inventory of the areas in your life where you are weak. We all have areas that we need to upgrade our skill levels. Do not be afraid to admit weak areas and work on a solution to improve those weaknesses. What areas do you need to improve and what areas do you need to acquire a skill you currently do not have. Nascar racing is a good example of the need to acquire skill. An average person could take a regular race car on the track and drive successfully at about 140 miles per hour, but a trained race care driver would be able to push the same car up to 180 - 200 miles per hour. What is the difference. Simply a learned skill that takes practice to perfect. What skill/s will you need to acquire or improve that you do or do not have at this time. God has given you supernatural abilities, natural abilities and He can give you opportunities for improvement or acquisition of a skill.

Make a list of areas you need to improve.

_____

_____

Make a list of skills you need to acquire.

_____

_____

_____

Key Question: What has God given You in Spiritual Gifts, Natural Abilities and Past Experiences and Skills?

_____

_____

_____

Action Item

Are you using these gifts in pursuit of your vision? Start moving today in pursuit of your dream from God. Set a time frame with a statement like this; In in the next ____ years I will _____

_____

_____

Prophetic word: *My grace is sufficient for you. My grace supplies all you need to become like me. My grace is my power supply to enable you to do all things in me. I am the God of the impossible and yes even the improbable. Expect unusual things in your life because I live inside of you. I am the very grace you need to live in my life and power.*

HELPFUL RESOURCES

The Nature of Freedom by Graham Cooke

Chapter 10
Placement and People in the Kingdom.

Key Scripture : Nehemiah 1:2 *That Hanani, one of my brethren, came, he and certain men of Judah; and I asked them concerning the Jews that had escaped, which were left of the captivity, and concerning Jerusalem.*

Finding Your Place in the Kingdom

Nehemiah had a specific call to go back to Jerusalem. He also had a specific people he was called to help. He wanted to help his brothers at Jerusalem to rebuild the walls of protection for security. Everyone that is born in the kingdom of God has a specific call to a specific place and a specific people. In the parable of the tares of the field, Jesus makes it clear the importance of a man sowing in his field. He later explains the meaning of the parable and the field the man sowed into as being in the world. Jesus always calls us to the people He desires to reach.

*Another parable put he forth unto them, saying, The kingdom of heaven is likened unto a man which sowed good seed **in his field** (Matthew 13:24)*

In the Kingdom of God we must determine what field we are called to minister so we can be effective to reap when we sow in the proper field. In the parable of the mustard seed, it is very clear that the seed must be sown in the proper field.

*Another parable he put forth unto them, saying, the kingdom of heaven is like to a grain of mustard seed, which a man took, and sowed **in his field.** (Matthew 13:31)*

We see the same principle in the story of the pearl of great price and in the treasure in the field, Jesus makes it clear the importance of a man having his own specific field.

Again the kingdom of heaven is like unto treasure hid in a field; the which when a man hath found, he hideth, and for joy thereof goeth, and selleth all that he hath, and buyeth that field.

*Again the kingdom of heaven is like unto a merchant man, seeking goodly pearls; Who when he had found one pearl of great price, went and sold all that he had and bought it.(**Matthew 13:44-46**)*

When we find the field we are called to minister into, we begin to blossom in the purposes of God. Nehemiah was certain of his placement in the plans of God. Jerusalem was were he felt called to go. Jerusalem was clearly the field of God's calling. I have had several members of my churches who are quite bored with going to church. They would at times be quite vocal about this. Sometimes I would be slightly irritated about this and would try in a smooth way to correct them. One day the light went on, and I began to realize the reason they were bored is because they had a heart for the lost and wanted to be out on the streets. Instead of me heaping guilt on them, I commissioned them to go and evangelize. They were called to spend most of their time with the lost. Paul had specific instructions of where he was called to minister.

*For so hath the Lord commanded us,(saying), I have set thee to be a light of the Gentiles, that thou shouldest be for salvation unto the ends of the earth. (**Acts 13:47**)*

Paul was called to the Gentiles. You also will have a specific calling. These callings help to keep us focused on God's specific assignment, keeping us from being distracted with things God has not designed for us to walk in. Another word often used for the field we are called to operate in, is our sphere of influence. Our sphere of influence is the place where we effectively operate as ambassadors for Christ Kingdom.When we understand our role in the Kingdom of God, we realize that everywhere we go, we are representing what the King is like. The power of the King helps us to be like Him and do what He does. Our sphere of influence is our everywhere we operate. Remember that your everywhere is different than my everywhere. When finding where your sphere of influence is located, a helpful tool is being able to pick which area you are called to influence. Knowing the field, where you will sow is essential for understanding and discovering your vision. A farmer does not sow in another persons farm, but the farm he operates or owns. You must understand the field that God has called you to sow. When you are sowing in the wrong field, it is easy to develop a sense of uneasiness. You might have a gut feeling that something is not right. Spend time with the Lord and get clarity that the field you are operating in is God ordained. Being in the right place at the right time is vital for operating in God's perfect plan. We had an old saying in Seminary when we would see the new students come for a new semester and it went like this, *some are momma sent, some are papa sent, some are God sent, and some just up and went.* Make sure you are God sent.

There are many ways to categorize these fields. These fields are often called domains or spheres of influence. Whether we call these areas domains or mountains of influence, this will help us with laser focus to find our field. *Dr Lance Wallnau*, from the Lance Learning Group, describes the 7 Spheres of Influence as :

Media,

Government,

Business,

Family,

Church/Ministry,

Education

Arts/Entertainment.

Two spiritual giants in the faith, Loren Cunningham, founder of Youth with a Mission, and Bill Bright, founder of Campus Crusade for Christ, were the originators of this concepts of the seven mountains.

They both wanted to serve others in reaching them with the Love of Christ.

Dave Beuhring, founder of Lionshare and the author of the book, *The Jesus Blueprint*, call these areas, the 12 domains, which include the following areas;

Family and Social Services,

Church and Missions,

Government Law and Nation Security,

Education and Students,

Electronic Print and Digital Media,

Arts, Entertainment and Sports,

Business and Commerce,

Science and Technology,

Health and Medicine,

Environment, Agriculture and Zoology,

Non- Profits and Service Organizations,

Peoples (affinity/culture kinship).

Whether you use the seven spheres or the twelve domains, it helps to have clarity in the field you are called to influence. Let me make it abundantly clear from some critics who mock the concept of influencing culture. We are not called to dominate people, we are called to serve people. In order to serve people we have to penetrate areas of society, to actually touch people. Jesus had a clear calling in His mission statement found in Luke chapter 4.

The Spirit of the Lord is upon me, because he hath annointed me to preach the gospel to the poor; he hath sent me to heal the brokenhearted, to preach deliverance to the captives, and recovering of sight to the blind, to set at liberty them that are bruised, To preach the acceptable year of the Lord. ***(Luke 4:18-19)***

He was called to the poor, brokenhearted, captive, blind, and the bruised. Notice He was anointed for this purpose. We are anointed for our purpose. We must also understand that our field will always be in the world. In the parable of the tares, Jesus clearly explains in Matthew 13:38 that the field is in the world and the good seed is the children of the Kingdom. We are the seed sown in our field of influence.

The church in America has been hibernating and hiding in our own little clubs. We are either hibernating from our culture or penetrating culture. Do not try to intimidate others but have a servant's heart for others. The world desperately needs those with servant hearts willing to help those who even do not want any help. We have been in isolation and the culture has totally degraded into a total mess. Come out of hiding my Beloved and let Jesus use you as a servant in our society, not to control but to influence those around us for Jesus and His love.

My calling was very clear at a fairly young age during college, as I was called to a fivefold ministry at the age of 20. My area of influence was the Ministry/Church mountain. Remember I still had strong influence on the Family mountain as I raised 4 kids. As far as my God given calling it was clear I was called to the Church/Ministry area. We must remember we have different seasons in our lives which help to determine our primary calling at certain times and seasons in our lives.

Let me tell you a story about a young lady who had a eye wakening moment in Church during a sermon I presented. About thirteen years ago, as I was teaching from the book on Nehemiah on finding your assignment or purpose, I presented the 7 Spheres of Influence listed above. During the message a light came on in her heart. After the sermon, she came up to me with tears in her eyes, and she said and I quote, " *I always felt guilty about not doing more in the church even though I have many skills I can use in helping the church. But deep down I always felt my place was to be home and minister to my family and my special needs daughter. After your sermon, I understand that my sphere of influence primarily is my family."* This sister was overcoming a load of guilt and shame, by simply understanding the place she was called to influence. God has a specific field for you. Stop right now and settle this in your heart. Let God speak to you. Do not fall prey to the enemies deceit of putting guilt and shame on you because you are not called to be in church twenty four hours a day. We as Pastors and leaders in the Body of Christ can heap quilt on our parishioners, when we demand they serve the church more to help us build our own kingdoms. Our primary purpose as Pastors should be to help people find their vision, not guilt them with helping us build our vision. You can go into a mega church and simply ask the people in the congregation what is your life vision. Most likely 90% will not have a clue what is their God given life vision. This can also be true in a small church. We are failing as leaders if we are not helping the saints in the pews to find their life callings. We need our churches filled with passionate workers called to their sphere of influence, walking in the power of the Holy Spirit. Take some time in the Lord's presence to settle which sphere of influence you are called to at this time. Feel free to ask for help in answering this question.

Key Question: What is the field you are called to influence? Pick one and describe why.

For the sake of simplicity I will use the 7 spheres model.

Area X

Family _____

Business _____

Church/Ministry _____

Media _____

Government _____

Arts/Entertainment _____

Education _____

Other, please describe :

_____

_____

_____

For assistance in finding your field or sphere of influence go to our website: www.thevisionprinciple.com

Finding the people you are called to.

As we discover our sphere of influence, we also need to understand the type of people we are called to minister unto in our sphere. This will help us to fine tune our God given vision, as God always gives us a vision for the benefit of other people. If you feel called to the business mountain, what type of people do you want to affect. Yes you might desire to make money, but what is the purpose for that money. If you have no significant purpose, what is the point of the money. I have met several people who have had a dream to be a millionaire before a certain age. Their reason for wanting to be a millionaire is self centered and not driven by a Godly passion. Needless to say they have not been very successful.This is a life without any meaning and significance. God has a heart for people and He has put His heart in us. If you have a vision for playing golf every day then your vision is self centered and not a God given vision that is centered on helping people. God is not against us playing golf, but He has a specific call for each one of us that involves much more than simply recreation. Below is a list of different types of people we might be called to help. Pick the one that is burning inside your heart. Maybe there will be more than one area. As you go through this list, it will become more and more clear to your heart.

Children	Men	Single People
Teenagers	Parents	College Students
Women	Single Parents	Career Professionals

Business People	Handicapped People	Mentally Ill
Homeless People	Prisoners	Seniors
Unemployed People	Immigrants	Nursing Home
Christians	Drug Addicts	Poor People
Non Christians	Prostitutes	Sick People

Other explain: _____

You might have circled two or three areas. Look at the areas you circled and it will become clear there is a pattern. If you circled women, prostitutes and mentally ill, then you clearly are beginning to know who you are called to. God has put that desire inside your redeemed heart. Listen to His voice as He wants to speak to you clearly. When you identify an area, ask the Lord to help you to be even more specific. For example, you might feel called to women, but also answer the question what type of women.

*And when he putteth forth his own sheep, he goeth before them, and the sheep follow him: for they know his voice. (**John 10:4**)*

If we belong to Jesus, we have the ability to hear His voice if we will take time to listen. Also the Lord will go before us, as He will not ask us to do anything, that He himself has not already done. We might be fearful or intimidated with the calling God has given us. Jesus is the confidence we need, because He lives in us and we can surely rely on Him.

Being confident of this very thing, that he which hath begun a good work in you will perform it until the day of Jesus Christ. **(Philippians 1:6)**

Our confidence is in God who is working in us before He works through us. Start spending time with the people that God has put on your heart, so you can develop the ministry of your calling.

Key Question: What type of people do you feel called to help?

_____

_____

_____

Action item.

Find the type of people you feel called to help and look for local opportunities to spend time with them, even on a voluntary basis. This will help solidify your call.

Prophetic Word: *You already have a burden in your heart to reach a certain group of my people. The love you have for them is from me. I will intensify this burden in the future as you will know I am calling you to touch them with my love. Listen to me, I am speaking to you about this. Do not let others sidetrack you. Hear my voice and begin to move toward these people with my love. I will help you to love them the way I love them. Do not be afraid, I am with you in all things.*

HELPFUL RESOURCES

Vision Assessment Tool by Jack B. Irvin Sr.
Destiny Finder by Michael Brodeur

....

Chapter 11
Planning to stay on task.

Key Scripture: Habakkuk 2:2 *And the Lord answered me, and said, Write the vision and make it plain upon the tables , that he may run that readeth it. For the vision is yet for an appointed time, but at the end it shall speak, and not lie:though it tarry, wait for it; because it will surely come, it will not tarry.*

Purpose without a plan is not a dream but a pipe dream. You will never fulfill your purpose without a plan. This plan must include action items that you will do on a regular basis to fulfill your God given vision. Scripture tells us *man devises a plan and the Lord directs his steps.*You need to write down the vision that God has given you. The Lord instructed Habakkuk to write the vision down and make it plain. We need to write down what God has placed in our hearts.This is what we call a vision statement. Some would call this strategic planning. In order to come up with a clear concise plan, you need to describe clearly what the big picture looks like and then develop specific step by step action plans or goals to achieve your vision. Once you do the vision statement you can begin to write a mission statement which will describe the specific things you will do living out your vision.

First let us look at the components of a good vision statement. Writing a life vision statement can be quite challenging.This vision statement should include the following: Purpose which should include your title, pain that you strongly want to help others overcome, passion for what you love to do, power that God has given you, (both spiritual and natural strengths), past experiences you can use to help with the vision, the place and people you are called to help, a specific time to operate in your vision. This statement should be birthed in spending time in the Lord's presence and in prayer. Toward the end of this chapter you will begin to write your own vision statement.

Years ago I played a lot of tennis. And I learned quite quickly that if you hit the tennis ball in the sweet spot the ball has great velocity and accuracy. The key though to hitting the ball in the sweet spot was not just the swing, but the preparation before the swing. The preparation of the body and the feet before the swing, determined the chance of hitting the ball in the sweet spot. I also coached players who consistently wanted to hit the ball in the sweet spot but would not take the time to make the effort to position their bodies and feet properly. They just wanted to swing without any preparation. Planning is like the preparation, so you can hit the ball properly. If you just want to take a swing at your life without preparation, you will have limited success. Planning experts tell us for every 10 minutes of planning, you will save hours of execution.

Our lives are multifaceted and require goals for each area of our lives. Paul had a goal that motivated him to follow the plan that Jesus had for him to preach the unsearchable riches of the Gospel.

I press toward the mark for the prize of the high calling of God in Christ Jesus.(Philippians 3:14)

Take time regularly to set goals for specific areas of your life before the start of each year. Whether you are doing what is called a life assessment, or new year resolutions, make sure you have clearly defined goals for the following areas listed below. A good resource for setting goals is the website http://stunningmotivation.com. Make these goals, SMART goals. Specific, Measurable, Accurate, Realistic, and a Timetable. Let me remind you that you can set goals each year, but not really achieve any of these goals. You must clearly focus on the process that will help you achieve your goals and the task or assignments necessary to that end. A good resource that will be helpful is Todd Herman, the creator of *90 Day Year High Performance System.*

Do you understand that each one of us needs to be disciplined in every area of our lives. We can understand our life vision but still have so many areas in our lives that are out of order. This can cause us to feel like total failures because of some area in our life that is totally out of control. Planning should not only involve plans for us to fulfill our God given vision, but also include a plan for every area of our lives. Dr David Jeremiah says,"Don't wait until the moment of crisis. plan ahead, hide God's word in your heart, and pray in advance for victory, holiness, and a life pleasing to God." One major area out of control can cause catastrophic damage resulting in us not being able to fulfill our heavenly calling. Many experts have developed what is often called the circle of life or the wheel of life. No matter what we label this, the most important thing is do you have a plan for the key areas of your life. I have chosen seven main areas that we need a real plan to help insure wholeness or balance. The seven areas are:

1. Faith.

2. Family and Friends.

3. Freedom.

4. Fitness-Mental&Physical.

5. Fun.

6. Function.

7. Finances

Let's assess how you are doing in these 7 areas with some key questions. On a scale of 1-10.

1 being weak and 10 being strong. Circle where you are on these key questions.

LIFE ASSESSMENT

1. Faith.

	weak								strong	
Do you have a vibrant relationship with God?	1	2	3	4	5	6	7	8	9	10
Are you spending daily time in God's presence?	1	2	3	4	5	6	7	8	9	10
Do you spend time in the word daily?	1	2	3	4	5	6	7	8	9	10

2. Family and Friends

How are your family
relationships?
1 2 3 4 5 6 7 8 9 10

Do you have a healthy relationship 1 2 3 4 5 6 7 8 9 10
with someone of the same sex to
be accountable with?

Do you have strong fellowship
with others?
1 2 3 4 5 6 7 8 9 10

Do have a strong intimate
relationship with your Spouse?
1 2 3 4 5 6 7 8 9 10

3. Freedom

Are you experiencing spiritual
freedom in your thought life?
1 2 3 4 5 6 7 8 9 10

Do you have a habit you can not
overcome?
1 2 3 4 5 6 7 8 9 10

Do you have a clear understanding 1 2 3 4 5 6 7 8 9 10
of who you are in Christ?

4. Fitness - Mental- Physical

Do you on a regular basis read
inspiring books?
1 2 3 4 5 6 7 8 9 10

Do you have someone who
mentors you to improve?
1 2 3 4 5 6 7 8 9 10

| Do you have a regular exercise routine? | 1 2 3 4 5 6 7 8 9 10 |

5. Fun

Do you take time to enjoy leisure activities you enjoy?	1 2 3 4 5 6 7 8 9 10
Have you eliminated wasteful time of too much leisure?	1 2 3 4 5 6 7 8 9 10
Do you regular take time to spend with your family enjoying what recreational activities they like?	1 2 3 4 5 6 7 8 9 10

6. Function

Do you have a healthy atmosphere in your work career?	1 2 3 4 5 6 7 8 9 10
Have you identified your heavenly calling?	1 2 3 4 5 6 7 8 9 10
Do you have a commitment to a local church or body where you help others and serve?	1 2 3 4 5 6 7 8 9 10

7. Finances

Are you own a regular controlled budget?	1 2 3 4 5 6 7 8 9 10
Do you have a plan to eliminate debt?	1 2 3 4 5 6 7 8 9 10
Have you identified your revenue streams?	1 2 3 4 5 6 7 8 9 10

Take time to analyze the results. The lower the score is an indication of a weakness. The higher score and indication of strength. Notice the areas you are weakest and come up with a plan to improve these areas. Ask for help if needed. You need to come up with goals for each one of these areas. Try to design a simple one page goal sheet that you can look at on a daily basis. Put it by your calendar or a place of easy access. These goals should include both long term and short term goals. These goal should be SMART GOALS. Specific, Measurable, Accurate, Realistic, and Timeable. Sample goals below:

- I will read 4 books this year.

- I will eliminate by credit card balances of $4,000 by June 2019, by paying 400 per month.

- I will lose 15 pounds in the next 8 months.

- I will save 15% each month of my total salary.

Below is a sample goal sheet. You can download a free Planning Guide to help with your planning for your life vision at www. thevisionprinciple.com under the resources tab.

Vision Goals Sheet
(Include a completion date if applicable)

Faith Goals

1. _____

2. _____

3. _____

Family and Friends

1. _____

2. _____

3. _____

Freedom

1. _____

2. _____

3. _____

Fitness Mental

1. _____

2. _____

3. _____

Fitness Physical

1. _____

2. _____

3. _____

Fun

1. _____

2. _____

3. _____

Function

1. _____

2. _____

3. _____

Finances

1. _____

2. _____

3. _____

Writing a Vision and Mission Statement

An important aspect of planning is the need to write a clear and concise vision and mission statement. In order to take specific steps in fulfilling your God given vision, you must have a clear understanding of the big picture. The vision statement is the big picture description of what you want to do. Your mission statement will be more of a specific statement on things you will actually do. Again if you want more detail go to my website under resources and purchase the vision assessment tool at www.thevisionprinciple.com.

Your vision statement should include the time frame for when you will begin to walk in your God given vision, a description of your title, and the people you will help, taking into consideration your power factor which includes your spiritual gifts, natural abilities and past experiences. You will also need to understand your personality as this will help you identify the people and the place you are called to. This statement will include your pain factor which will motivate you to solve the number 1 problem you will help others overcome. In most cases this should be written in the future tense. Use this template below to help you write the vision statement.

In the next _____, or starting immediately,

Time Frame

As a _____, I will _____

_____,

Passion/Title Action you will take and the problem you will solve _____, _____

_____

People you will help, your field Result you desire to see achieved

If needed supported by, _____

_____

How you will be supported financially

Rewrite your vision statement in the below blanks:

_____

_____

_____

_____

_____

_____

Examples of a Vision Statement

"As a Pastor, Teacher, Coach, Consultant, Trainer, Author and Speaker, I will train, equip and motivate individual believers to define, discover and develop their God given vision for their lives, and turn their passion into a simple lifestyle income when needed, teaching them to walk in their called sphere of influence in the Kingdom of God, by the power of the Holy Spirit, conformed to the image of Jesus"

In the next 3-5 years, as a Pastor of a local street church in Cleveland, I will teach, train and counsel drug addicts and street people through, bible studies, church, halfway houses, rehabilitation centers, how to overcome addictions and to restore them to a healthy lifestyle with their family, church and community, as devoted followers of Jesus, supported by the local church, grant funding, my personal income from work and business and donations from other churches, ministries and members of the body of Christ.

When you write your vision statement, share it with reputable people who are partners with you, such as your Pastor or spiritual advisors. Please use some wisdom as to who you share this with, as there will be many dream stealers that will respond in a negative way. Place this vision statement in a prominent place and refer back to this statement on a regular basis. Feel free to email me also, if you would like input on your statement at pastorjack@thevisionprinciple.com

Key Question: Do you know where you are going and how you will get there?

_____

_____

_____

Action Item: Writing a mission statement.

Begin to write out a mission statement below, which should include your title/s, the people you will serve, the location and name if possible, the problem you will solve, and the result you desire to achieve. List specific services you will offer. This will be placed on your personal website and promotional materials. Write this in the present tense.

_____

_____

_____

Example of a mission statement

"As a Pastor, Teacher, Trainer, Coach, Consultant, Author, and Speaker, I will equip, train and motivate individual Christians in a local church and the body of Christ, to define, discover and develop their God given vision for their lives and churches, using Books, and E-Books, CD's, DVD's, Videos, Seminars, Guest Speaking, Church Meetings, Retreats, Bible College, Home Fellowship Groups, Discipleship Groups, teaching them to walk in their called sphere of influence in the Kingdom of God, walking in the power of the Holy Spirit, being conformed to the image of Jesus."

Having a vision and mission statement will be helpful to keep you focused on the task and assignment God has given uniquely to you. These are the big picture tools. With these you can begin to write a detailed specific plan of how you will accomplish these statements. Let the work begin.

Prophetic word: *Do not be afraid to call yourself what I am calling you. My Plans for you are what I created in you before the foundation of the world. Do not let others intimidate you, as you are secure in my calling. Rest in my Power to help you to be all I have planned for you. My plan is a heavenly plan that will satisfy your soul. When you walk with me, you will know me and the path you should walk without fear or anxiety. Trust in me. I know what is best for you.*

HELPFUL RESOURCES

The Rest of Your Life by Patrick Morley
Planning Guide by Pastor Jack Irvin Sr at www.
thevisionprinciple.com

Chapter 12
Practical Considerations

Key Scripture: Nehemiah 2:1 *And it came to pass in the month Nisan, in the twentieth year of Artaxerxes the king, that wine was before him: and I took up the wine, and gave it unto the king. Now I had not been before-time sad in his presence.*

Price to pay.

Nehemiah risked his very life by being sad before the king. Fulfilling your vision will cost you everything. Every vision will require a death to selfish ambition, work on character development issues and a deeper devotional relationship with Jesus. We must be willing to pay whatever price we have to pay. Paul suffered the loss of all things that he might when the prize of the high call of Jesus.

Yea doubtless,and I count all things but for the loss for the excellency of the knowledge of Christ Jesus my Lord: for whom I have suffered the loss of all things and do count them but dung, that I may win Christ. **(Philippians 3:8)**

Are you willing to pay the price? Are you willing to sell all you have to purchase the field that God is calling you to, just like the story in the pearl of great price? Throughout the vision process there will be great challenges and obstacles to overcome. You must be willing to stay committed no matter what happens. You will not be able to always take the easy road with little commitment and no pain or suffering. Paul did most of the writing of the New Testament in prison in Rome. Jesus had to suffer great agony on the cross to bring many sons and daughters to their salvation.

Patience and persistence to endure.

Persistence and patience are valuable commodities to possess in vision fulfillment. Living a life of purpose is not a instant event without a period of time and patience. Living in a society of instant gratification can hinder our need to slow down and wait on God's perfect timing in our calling and assignments. The journey is as important as the destination. Jesus is working in us long before he works through us. He wants us to be a *vessel of honor fit for the master's use*. Moses had to wait 40 years in the desert before the time of his calling materialized. Jesus, God Almighty in the flesh, had to wait 30 years before he began his 3 1/2 year ministry on earth.

For ye have need of patience, that, after ye have done the will of God, ye might receive the promise. **(Hebrews 10:36)**

Priorities must be maintained

Everything in the Kingdom of God has to be in right priority. We must seek first the Kingdom of God. Things in this life come and go, but God is eternal and worthy to be placed first in our lives. First before family, first before money, first before ministry, first before relationships and yes even first before church, or religious activities. He is first.

But seek ye first the Kingdom of God, and his righteousness; and all these things shall be added unto you. **(Matthew 6:33)**

Let me remind all of us that achieving great things for God will never replace the need for operating in humility for God. We need to be like Him in all we say and do. Lord help us today to be filled with your love and your priority each and every day.

Prayer in private brings power in public.

We should have a private time of devotion with God in prayer each day. We can easily get so busy fulfilling the will of God, that we forget to spend time with God. If your life is constantly filled with busyness, you are missing the special time in His presence that brings real satisfaction to the soul.

And when you pray, do not be like the hypocrites, for they love to pray standing in the synagogues and on the street corners to be seen by others. Truly I tell you, they have received their reward in full. (Matthew 6:5)

Profits the ideal benefit.

If it is possible, when you discover your vision and begin to actually walk in your vision, an ideal benefit would be you are able to generate a simple lifestyle income that is related to your vision. If you are called to Pastor, ideally you can have a income that is sufficient for your family needs. If you are in the marketplace, a sustainable, sufficient income is a blessing. There are some things we can do to achieve this. Some already have a source of revenue especially those who have retired. In my own case, For many years, I have been what is called a bi-vocational minister. Another words, I have had a full time job and I did ministry part time. This scenario can be challenging for family life. I have been a church planter, starting churches without sponsorships or backing from a denomination. In a case like this, you have to gradually raise money to plant a church. Provision is what God provides when we live in our life vision. God does this in many ways, whether we be part time or bi-vocational, or full time in our calling. Are you willing to do what it takes to live your life vision, making whatever sacrifice you need to make. If you are not willing to do this, then you will not see the fulfillment of your God given vision. Many people have great dreams but they do not have the discipline to sacrifice and stay committed when the going gets tough. You must be relentless in pursuit of your passion and purpose. The graveyards are filled with people who live with regret because they were not willing to pay the price to achieve their vision.

It is possible to generate an income, while at the same time fulfilling your life calling whether it be in ministry or the marketplace. Some experts calls this monetizing your message. This can be a difficult thing to do, as we need spiritual wisdom, not worldly wisdom to realize financial support and at the same time achieve our God given dream. We do not want to fall into the trap of manipulating or merchandising people to financially support us for the wrong reasons. But it is clearly biblical to ask for support to fulfill your ministry to others.

Even so hath the Lord ordained that they which preach the gospel should live of the gospel. **(1 Corinthians 9:16)**

You do not need to beg or manipulate people to support you. Those you minister to will want to support you because of what you have poured into their lives. It is possible to have a reasonable income as a Pastor, although you might have to supplement your income in other ways. If your ministry is to the Body of Christ, it is appropriate to ask for financial support as a missionary. You can also provide goods and services on a reasonable basis to generate revenue streams. Understand that it is not how much money you make, as it is about how much money you need. I have seen so many saints not be able to respond to the call of God because they were so much in debt and enslaved to a job they hated. Chose to live a simple lifestyle and be a good steward of what God has already given you. If you are not faithful with mammon, how can you be faithful with the true riches of the Gospel. But your goal should not be to become rich at the expense of others.

Remember a Dream with a Theme will have a Team that produces a Stream. There are many ways to generate income, so you can live the life God is calling you to. When He gives vision, He will provide. What is your financial plan to ensure you can fulfill what God is calling you to do? This plan should include ideas to generate revenue and ways to eliminate debt.Write down a clear plan. Make sure you involve the mentor/s you have chosen, who is doing what you want to do. How are they supported? What sacrifices have they made? Get some coaching from someone who can assist with this plan. Contact me at my email pastorjack@thevisionprinciple.com and we can look at possibly coaching or assisting in this area.This area is too in depth to cover in this book, but it is possible to monetize your message and to develop a strategy to generate revenue for your God given vision. Become an author, produce CD's and DVD's, start coaching and consulting in your area of expertise, start an online business, buy a producing asset with investment money that is earning a small yield, do affiliate marketing using other peoples products.

Some great resources that can help with this area are the following;

Tamara Lowe, *Kingdom Builders Academy Boot Camp* at www. kingdombuilders.com and also Lance Wallnau, *Ninja Marketing*, at www.lancewallnau.com.

Practical practices

Take time to start a book or file or folder on your vision which will include specific areas you will need to addressed. Make a master checklist of action items which you need to accomplish. Have the checklist be practical areas you know will need to be address.

Below are some items you will need on that checklist. Some of you are great organizers, so use your imagination. Others of you are not good organizers, so this will be of great benefit to you.
Below is a sample checklist.

Vision Checklist
(Fill in with pencil as things will change)

Legal	Completion	Time Frame	Cost
Name			
Ein Number			
Checking Account			
LLC non-profit			
501 3C			
Constitution and Bylaws			
Technical			
Website Development			
Website Developer			
Online Donations Capability			

Website Hosting   _____   _____   _____

Facebook Page   _____   _____   _____

Twitter Account   _____   _____   _____

Instagram Account   _____   _____   _____

Twitter Account   _____   _____   _____

Financial

Fundraising   _____   _____   _____

Accounting System   _____   _____   _____

Administrative

Board Development   _____   _____   _____

Communication   _____   _____   _____

Spiritual

Prayer warriors   _____   _____   _____

Pastor covering   _____   _____   _____

Mentors   _____   _____   _____

Other (Fill in the Blank)

_____   _____   _____   _____

_____   _____   _____   _____

_____   _____   _____   _____

_____   _____   _____   _____

_____   _____   _____   _____

_____   _____   _____   _____

Keep this checklist in a folder so you can on a regular basis check theses items. Make it personal for your specific action plans. This is just a guide to get you started.

You can go to the website and download this checklist as part of the Free Planning Guide at www.thevisionprinciple.com

Practical Benefits of Vision

There are many benefits to having a clear God given vision. People with vision know where they need to go. People without vision seem to wander aimlessly in life, not having a sense of direction. Below is a list of the benefits of vision. Make up your mind today to be one who understands their destiny and has a commitment to fulfill God's plan.

Vision brings Focus	**Vision brings Discipline**
Vision brings Clarity	**Vision brings Opportunity**
Vision brings Purpose	**Vision brings Uniqueness**
Vision brings Hope	**Vision brings Passion**
Vision brings Life	**Vision brings Significance**
Vision brings Priorities	**Vision brings Persistence**

Key Question : Do you have a practical checklist with action items you need to take to achieve your God given vision? Do your checklist today.

Action Item: Start today to identify the most important thing you can do to start moving towards fulfilling your God given vision. Make your heavenly vision a priority.

Prophetic word: *The essence of sin is missing the mark of what I have ordained that you should walk in. You can decide today to walk with me and be like me, and do what I want you to do because I am in you. Keep your focus on me, keep your heart turned towards me. Bring all your failures to me and I will shew you mercy. My perfect love cast out all fears. You are my beloved.*

There is nothing more you can do to get me to love you more. Rest in my love and lean unto my everlasting arms. I will always hold you up in your time of need.

HELPFUL RESOURCES

The Nature of Freedom by Graham Cooke

Conclusion

The Dream

About 10 years ago, I had a very vivid dream during the night that was clearly from the Lord. I remembered in great detail the specifics of the dream. I was in the middle of ministering to a local church that was in great division and needed help to heal and move forward. I had been asked by another leader in the Body of Christ to help this troubled church. This dream was not directed to this church in particular, but I believed directed to the Body of Christ as a whole.

The dream began with me walking into an old school with a great big auditorium, and there was a lady in charge and the Lord told me to tell her she was suspended. I told her what the Lord said and she looked quite surprised and troubled. I immediately walked down the hallway of the school and came to what looked like the music room and this room was vast in size. I sat down in the room and one of my mentors was in the room with me. He began to lay hands on me and the scene was quite unusual. On top of my head was a bullseye with an arrow pointed right in the middle. My mentor prayed for me and I immediately got up and walked over to a piano in the room and began to play with an incredible anointing. All at once, children from every direction began to gather around me at the piano with great joy and excitement as I began to play. I immediately woke up from the dream remembering all the details.

When God speaks to us, sometimes we have difficulty understanding what He is saying. When a dream or prophetic word comes we must understand it can have 3 distinct parts; the dream or word, the interpretation, and the application. These three areas normally involve a period of time so the word or dream can manifest and develop and for us to have a clear understanding of what God is saying. After this dream, I had tremendous clarity as to what this meant for me personally and corporately for the Body of Christ. The old school represented the church were people were being trained and instructed.The lady represented the control of Jezebel over the church and the large auditorium represented the vast influence and control Jezebel has had over the Body of Christ, me telling her she is suspended is the Lord sending me and a vast army to expose and expel her from control, the hallway represents the journey we are on to find our destiny and purpose in God, the music room vast in size represents the Kingdom of God and it expansion, the mentor is a needed ingredient for us to find our destiny, the bullseye with the target represents the vision each one of us should have, the piano represents the desires of our hearts that God has placed inside us, and the children coming from every direction represents the effect each one of us will have to influence people and set them free as we walk in our divine vision.

For too long the church has been training the saints to operate in the church, but not in the Kingdom. The Kingdom of God is not just the Body of Christ. The Kingdom of God is everywhere we go. This is not a finger pointing session at leaders who have done their best to try and equip people for the Lord. I know I personally have been part of the problem. We have tried to build our churches instead of teaching people how to operate in their real everyday lives. They can be involved in church activities, but they have no clue how to live in the Kingdom and their own sphere of influence. God has been speaking this to so many in the Body of Christ that we need to turn our focus to the Kingdom of God which operates 24 hours a day in us and away from the church focus we attend 2 hours a week. Let me also add that those who are unattached to a local church and ministering in other churches without a personal connection are fooling themselves. These folks would say they are kingdom minded, but in reality they are not willing to submit to anyones authority. We all need to be in submission to those who equip us for our ministries, not control us to build their empires. If possible, get connected to a local church and serve with those who are learning to come out of the church building and operate in the Kingdom 24 hours a day. Church is the training ground for the Kingdom. Your bullseye is your life calling and vision from God that you will operate in 24 hours a day as you walk with the King in the power of the Holy Spirit. I have always wanted to play the piano and this represents for me the desires of my heart that God has put inside of me. My greatest desire is to see all believers walk in their God given vision. This is the essence of the Vision Principle. God is raising up a mighty army of saints who want to walk in their God given visions. Would you like to break free from the control the enemy has had on you? Do you want to walk in your God given destiny? I break the power of the enemy over you this day. Be released into the divine plan Jesus has for you. Begin to walk in the power of God, filled with His purposes and flowing out of a heart of passion for your assignment and vision. Today is a new day. The cloud of confusion is leaving you and you are beginning to walk in His glorious light.

In conclusion, my wife loves to sing a hymn in the shower when no one is listening. She feels she is not a singer, so she likes to sing to the Lord alone. Her favorite hymn is "Be Thou My Vision". My wife heard this song at workout facility, being sung in the shower by an unseen person. When she got out of the shower she saw no one present. There is a good possibility this was an angel singing unto the Lord. This song spoke to her heart in a time of great sadness and gave her a fresh insight into the future healing the Lord would bring in her life. When she sings it, she has memorized every word. This hymn was believed to be written in the 8th century and translated by Eleanor Hull in 1912. This song is rooted in medieval Celtic Christianity and has grown very popular by modern Christian artists who have recorded the song. It is believed that the original poem may have been written by an Irish saint who experienced blindness later in life. Let this song speak to your heart.

> Be Thou my vision, O Lord of my heart
> Naught be all else to me, save that thou art
> Thou my best thought, by day or by night
> Waking or sleeping, thy presence my light
> Be thou my wisdom, and thou my true word
> I ever with thee and thou with me, Lord
> Thou my great Father; thine own may I be
> Thou in me dwelling and I one with thee

Be thou my battle shield, sword for my fight
Be thou my dignity, thou my delight
Thou my soul shelter and thou my high tower
Raise thou me heavenward , oh power of my power
Riches I heed not, nor man's, empty praise
Thou mine inheritance, now and always
Thou and thou only, first in my heart
High King of Heaven, my treasure thou art
High King of Heaven, my victory won,
May I reach heaven's joys, O bright heaven's sun
Heart of my own heart, whatever befall
Still be my vision, O ruler of all

In our pursuits of our God given vision, dream or assignments, we must always remember that Jesus is always the focus of our vision. Nothing else will satisfy our longing souls like Jesus. We can gain all the world and the things in this world and this will not fill the void we feel without Jesus being in the center. **HE IS OUR VISION. WE ARE COMPLETE IN HIM. WILL YOU LIVE BY THE VISION PRINCIPLE?**

And ye are complete in him, which is the head of all principality and power. *(Colossians 3:10)*

Discover Your Life Vision
Other Resources
You can find all these resource on the website
www.thevisionprinciple.com

The Vision Principle Study Guide by
Pastor Jack Irvin Sr. Great for group Bible studies

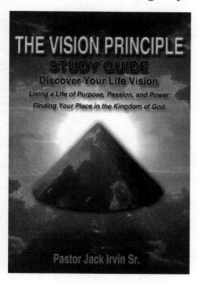

Daily Podcast, The Vision Principle, https://anchor.fm/jack-irvin-sr

Vision Planning Guide

Vision Assessment Tool for individuals

Weekly Group Coaching

One on One Coaching

Coming Soon, Vision Builders Academy, 90 Day Vision Builder Program

To schedule Pastor Jack for a Seminar or Retreat at your church

email me at pastorjack@thevisionprinciple.com

Made in the USA
Columbia, SC
02 April 2019